AFRICAN AMERICAN BRYAN TEXAS

AFRICAN AMERICAN BRYAN TEXAS

CELEBRATING THE PAST

OSWELL PERSON, PHD

Charleston London
THE History PRESS

Published by The History Press
Charleston, SC 29403
www.historypress.net

First published 2012
Revised edition, 2019

Manufactured in the United States

ISBN 978.1.60949.698.2

Library of Congress CIP data applied for.

CONTENTS

FOREWORD

Although Dr. Person has served as president and vice-president of several institutions of higher learning, he is more than an academic: he is also a historian. Dr. Person uses his inimitable ability to recall, not by rote but his interest and knowledge of individuals. Gregarious by nature, he takes the time to know people, ask them questions and learn about their families. I was his colleague a few years ago when he served as vice-president of an institution, and he amazed two hundred of his employees by learning all their names in just the first two weeks. In the sixty-five years that I have known him, he has demonstrated this gift time and time again. Today, he can even recall the names of all his first-grade classmates because he knew them well.

African American Bryan, Texas completes the work Person started in his book *Moving Forward from Behind* in 2011, which accurately chronicles African American life in Bryan, Texas. In his latest book, he focuses on a critical period after slavery but before affirmative action and federally mandated programs were instituted. There was no "war on poverty" then, just poverty. Although the time and setting coincide with life in the antebellum South, Person presents the antithesis of the idealized and romantic southern life as depicted in black literature.

Despite ever-present despair and apparent hopelessness, a surprising number of African Americans in Bryan persevered through hard work, ingenuity, education and family support. Today, successful blacks in Bryan stand on the shoulders of determined, hardworking pioneers who were ordinary but who were also high achievers, despite having meager resources.

Person acknowledges the contributions of other works on black Bryan but often found them to be inaccurate, inconsistent and incomplete. He stops short, however, of being overly critical, suggesting that these authors fulfilled their missions to summarize and approximate, and most of them did. After all, this history has long been omitted from most mainstream texts, and the conservative agenda of today's Texas State Board of Education has chosen to further purge textbooks of African American heritage.

Dr. Person's research took him directly to his sources, most of which were interviews with residents and their families and friends. He was able to connect with these subjects who may or may not know the value of their input. Rare and tucked-away photographs, as well as oral histories, were invaluable tools in recording and correcting events that are important in Bryan's history.

Person's strength and his quest for perfection drove him to examine, correct and record even minute details. For example, the history of one of Bryan's most prominent and successful families was corrected when Dr. Halcyon Watkins related that her dad, principal O.W. Sadberry Sr., was actually alive when Washington Elementary burned. This revelation was important because the school burned in 1970 (but was not rebuilt), the year before Bryan schools were fully integrated. Undoubtedly, Mr. Sadberry had a role in the process.

Like most history books, this book has no plot, and the author uses a familial approach to tell his story. Person recognized the family as the catalyst for survival and success in Bryan's African American community and often adds personal details about his family and his childhood. In one chapter, he describes the squalid conditions of living in "shotgun" houses and government projects and tells how his family escaped to their own newly built house not too far away. ("Shotgun" houses, of course, were houses with rooms directly in front of each other from front to back and were symbols of southern poverty.) White Bryan might have been oblivious to Person's black Bryan, with its shotgun houses, dry toilets, segregated and inadequate medical facilities and limited transportation; on that point, he is unclear. He does point out, however, that some Italian American business owners lived and did business in black neighborhoods, and some even hired his classmates to work for them. Several others owned businesses but lived in their own communities. Given the racial frenzy gripping present-day America, Person would have been justified to publish *Moving Forward*, but he did not. He neither decries the lack of justice nor bemoans the dearth of civil rights. In fact, he strikes an early, much-needed conciliatory tone: "Furthermore, I hope old wounds of individual treatment, unequal opportunities and impoverished living conditions have faded deeply into the background of our collective memories." This passage paves the way for a book that will appeal to more than just those whose stories are being told.

African American Bryan, Texas describes more than a resourceful people struggling to survive in a changing world amidst human drama and will evoke racial and regional pride, regardless of the reader's ethnicity. Furthermore, its recording and celebration of historical events and common black people with uncommon achievements can positively impact a cross section of society: Survivors, relatives and friends can appreciate, preserve and pass on to future generations a just chronicle of their recorded history; Teachers can study, take note and emulate "no-frill" methods used by their predecessors to motivate students; Youths of all backgrounds stand to be inspired by the accomplishments of so many who had so little; And finally, the multicultural community can improve racial harmony at all levels by gaining keen insight and understanding of the soul and grit of African Americans in Bryan.

African American Bryan loosens the veil of inclusion and invites individuals, organizations, governments and school districts throughout the Brazos Valley to step forward and celebrate the rich history of Bryan's African American community.

—Leroy Sterling

ACKNOWLEDGEMENTS

I would like to dedicate this book and give thanks to Dr. Constance Person (Connie), my wife; Vivian Peterson, my mother; and my principal at Washington Elementary School, Mr. Oliver Wayne Sadberry Sr., who made lasting impressions and incredible differences in my life.

First, to Connie, without whose love, success would not have been possible. She demonstrated support by leaving her professional job and house and moving into an apartment in married student housing at Michigan State University with her newborn son. After reestablishing her career in Michigan, she moved to California so I could advance my professional career, and then to North Carolina before spending eleven years relocating back and forth between Texas and Michigan, selling her house each time and buying a new one in whatever city we relocated to.

Second, to my mother, whose faith helped me to be strong and who taught me lessons to live by.

And finally, to Mr. Oliver W. Sadberry Sr., who never gave up on me and, in fact, invited me to come back and teach at Washington Elementary School in 1969. Unfortunately, I could not accept his invitation, as graduate school was in my immediate future.

A project of this scope could not have happened without the help of many other people. I want to offer my sincere gratitude and appreciation to the numerous individuals who have assisted in this project.

First, to my sons, Erick C. Person and Stephen D. Person, who have always supported me. A special thanks to Stephen for lending his computer skills to this project.

To my siblings, Betty, Pattie, Wanda and Waymon, who had the same early experiences in Bryan, Texas. Also to Waymon, who was an outstanding quarterback, served in Vietnam and provided names of other Vietnam veterans and members of his football team.

To my brother-in-law, Maurice Green Sr., who retired from his position as supervisor at the Bryan Sanitation Department after forty-five years. With his invaluable memory of city employees, he provided the first and last names of staff and their assigned departments. In addition, he was able to provide the full names of many World War II veterans. And to Wanda, for providing the names of her classmates who graduated from college and are now teachers. Both Maurice and Wanda made contributions that were profoundly significant and appreciated.

Thanks also to my first-grade classmates: Leroy Sterling, who wrote the foreword, shared books from his personal library and researched materials in the Brazos Valley African Museum and mailed them to me. He also agreed to be interviewed by local media outlets in Bryan and was of invaluable assistance with marketing and public relations. He also helped me remember businesses, events and people on the west side; To Dr. Halcyon Sadberry Watkins, for information on Bessie Matthews's place and the date of her father's death (December 4, 1970); To Sarah Greer Graham, for remembering the Italian American who owned the grocery store in her neighborhood; To Faye Thelma Patterson Sabbs, for providing names of Elijah Alonzo (E.A.) Kemp Junior-Senior High School college graduates from the classes of 1956, 1957 and 1958; To George Bell, who took messages and helped me to remember all the names of the E.A. Kemp "gang," including himself, brothers John, Sam and William (Will) Dunn, Willie Joe Kearney, James C. and Jon Mosley, R. (Reval) Newton and brothers Jimmy, Nelson and Pinkney Parnell (who, without fail, attended the Friday midnight movies at the segregated Palace Theater and sat in balcony seats); To Barbara Wilson Wright, for confirming names of Waco Street neighbors and the date Ollie Carter served in the military.

A special thanks to the late Mrs. Jessie Mae Walton for providing names of Dr. William A. Hammond Sr.'s children and their professions, for reminding me that her brother-in-law owned the grocery store on Waco Street and for reviewing the names of principals and teachers from 1885 to 1971. She made sure I knew the first names of the following Washington

Elementary School teachers: Mrs. Carter, Mrs. Cass and Mrs. Hall. She also introduced me to her classmate Berthenia Ellis Wallace, who also contributed useful information.

To the late James T. Murphy, for confirming the name of the boys' club founded by Oscar Pierce Sr. and the name of the Italian American who owned the grocery store on the corner of East Nineteenth and North Polk Streets. He also confirmed for me that Tommie M. Murphy has a master's degree, Vivian Murphy has a BSN and that he was the first African American to serve on the Victoria ISD Board.

Thanks to John Jerome Knox, for remembering that Lula was the first name of Mrs. Callier, my seventh-grade teacher. And to Rastine Calhoun, Iona Potts, Geraldine Adams and Tommy Traylor, all of whom helped confirm or remember names of football players and girls on the basketball teams.

To Ruby Ellis, for sharing the phone numbers of her classmates who could verify information sources. Thanks also to Rozell Quarles, for providing the names of cheerleaders, drill team members and majorettes from the classes of 1955, '56 and '57.

To James Knox, who reminded me that "Knox's Place," the most popular (and safe) recreational place for years, was converted to a rooming house.

To Velma Polk Allen, who faxed information on E.A. Kemp college graduates.

To Mildred Ross Phillips and Isaiah, who shared website information and a copy of the *Introductory Issue of John M. Moore Out-Look* (Volume One, 1946) and her prepared reunion document. She also confirmed the name of the African American grocery store owner on Twenty-eighth Street.

To Bobby Joe and Effie Perry, for inviting Constance and me into their home and providing names of college graduates, as well as for providing the names of teachers and athletic coaches who taught at R.C. Neal Junior High School and George Washington Carver Elementary School, the years E.A. Kemp High won district championships and use of their alumni directory.

To William G. Hall, who verified names of teachers and informed me he was an assistant principal at George Washington Elementary School, and confirming the first name of Walter Carr.

To members of the classes of 1945, '47 and '48: Clifton Greer, James Greer, Edward L. Colquitt, Rosie Greer and Marion "Buck" Williams, for helping to confirm names of their classmates.

To Adolph Johnson Jr., for confirming the names of his elementary, junior high and senior high school teachers, as well as those of his classmates who graduated from college. Thanks also for providing me with Linda Asberry's,

Robert Person's and Maurice Green Jr.'s phone numbers. And thanks to Jo Ann Jordan, who verified information sources and allowed me to use his yearbook.

To Ocie Hall Jr., for information about his uncle's café and father's employment at the Bryan Air Force Base.

To Irma Rooks Kearney, who supplied names of west side veterans and small business owners and a picture of the Galilee Church's a cappella choir.

Thanks to Bill Page, program coordinator for Research Services University Libraries, and to Texas A&M University staff for providing invaluable references and special assistance.

To Anne Boykin, a staff member at City of College Station, for information about her mother's research about Italian Americans.

Thanks to Nancy Ross, manager of the Carnegie Center of Brazos Valley History, and her staff, Ann Preston and Diane Smith, for their professional assistance with historical references and images of Bryan and for accepting and filling phone requests.

Thanks to Wayne Sadberry, curator, and staff member Velma Neblett Spivey at the Brazos Valley African American Museum, for information sources, photos and assistance.

To Martha Mosley Delley, for Carolyn Hammond Montier's phone number, from whom vital family information was obtained. Thanks to Dr. Carolyn H. Montier for confirming that her father, William A. Hammond Sr., was president of the African American Medical Association of Texas.

Thanks to citizens who read the billboard on Highway 6 entering the city that reads, "Bryan—The City with a Future" and pondered, as I do, "for whom?"

Thanks to George Vaults, for pictures of former E.A. Kemp basketball players and for reminding me the 1954 team was the runner-up in the state finals. Thanks to him also for sending his resume of accomplishments that include superintendent of Calvert ISD and being voted Superintendent of the Year in 1994 by Region VI.

Thanks to Shirley I. Knox Barnett, for confirming names of teachers at Washington Elementary School and for sharing picture of her father, Edward H. Knox, who was principal of Washington Elementary School from 1934 to 1943. And also to: James C. Mosley, for remembering the valedictorian of the class of 1953; Amos, for confirming the phone number of Melvin Turner; and Barbara F. Mosley Cooper, for sharing a photo of her father's venerable grocery store.

To Queen Esther Vaults Shaw, for professional career information about herself and her sister, Vivian Rawls; To Nettie Richardson Clay, who provided names of her classmates who taught public school; To Willie Taylor, who shared phone numbers and memories of E.A. Kemp classmates who attended Texas Southern University and also for personal stories of assistance from an Italian American family. Thanks also to "Blues Man" Nat Dove, for information about other Kemp alumni, sharing his many accomplishments and connecting me with other E.A. Kemp luminaries in music.

To Charles Nelson, who shared a personal photograph of his parents' café, and Christene Harris McQueen, for providing information about John M. Moore High School.

Thanks to Dr. Deborah Cowman, executive director of the Brazos Valley Museum of Natural History, for sharing the history of the oldest museum in Brazos Valley and for her willingness to sell books in the gift store. Thanks to Jon Isaacs, Roberta Kennedy, Greg Lee, Shawna McDaniels and Steve Mehalka, members of the CVS photo staff, who processed film and graciously assisted with transferring CD images.

They all deserve credit for their many contributions and have my deepest appreciation for their assistance. But I alone must take credit for any and all errors.

Author's commentary on revised edition:

I want to express thanks to individuals who helped in the search for new information about E.A. Kemp alumni and former students, making it possible for submission to publisher for consideration. Few efforts can be successful without assistance, and I extend thanks and appreciation to:

Dr. Constance Person, my wife for reading the first drafts.

Bobby Joe and Effie Perry for providing names of dozens of veterans. A special thanks to Effie for tireless searches for teachers, administrators and serving as editor in residence, 1956–66 E.A. Kemp alumni.

Carnegie Center of Brazos Valley history staff Joline Odell, for responding to phone calls, and Ann Preston, for searching for E.A. Kemp High School 1968 yearbook information.

As mentioned above, many individuals have assisted in efforts to include achievements and accomplishments of persons who contributed to the development of African American Bryan. Because so many individuals contributed in a variety of ways to helping African Americans survive humiliations, insults and injustices, all efforts have been made to be inclusive.

In conducting research for new information to be added to this book, teachers and others, who may not be E.A. Kemp alumni, were discovered and are included in this revised edition. They are included because their achievements are part of the legacy that contributed to the success of those who had to move forward from behind, and indicative of the legacy of African Americans in Bryan, Texas.

INTRODUCTION

The idea for this project began in 2008, at the E.A. Kemp High School business meeting for the class of 1949 reunion and the Decade of the Fifties E.A. Kemp alumni. One of the topics on the agenda was planning for the 2012 Bryan School for Colored and also for the E.A. Kemp High All School Reunion that traditionally occurs every five years (the last reunion was in August 2010). It was decided that since E.A. Kemp alumni were growing fewer and fewer every year, the reunion would be held every two years, beginning in 2012.

Originally, I thought of preparing a written account about African American life in Bryan from the years 1930 to 1971, about four decades before the 2010 All School Reunion. The idea started to take shape after I left the meeting. It soon became clear that in order to understand the conditions that set the stage for African American life in Bryan, it would be necessary to start much earlier than 1930. This book then starts in 1885, when the first public school for blacks was built, and ends in 1971, with the desegregation of schools. By doing so, I soon realized some events, people and places would most likely not be included in my first attempt. So I began my endeavor knowing that I owed an apology to many African American parents, students, teachers and other citizens who deserved to be included. It was certainly not my intent to offend anyone who bore the same experiences while trying to move forward from behind; someone will inevitably be left out of the period of time covered. But because so many individuals contributed in a variety of ways to helping African Americans survive the countless humiliations, insults and injustices and to move the city forward, every effort was made to be inclusive. I tried to include events, people and places that were not covered in my first book, and those that I missed this time will be included in a future history of Bryan.

Following the 2010 reunion, I had a conversation with Ann King, a graduate of Kemp High, and she told me about Simone Williams, who is an editor for Arcadia Publishing. Simone introduced me to Joseph Gartrell, special projects editor at The History Press, also a publisher of local and regional history. I thought if The History Press was interested in my topic, I would get the chance to include events and persons who were left out of the previous project.

Oftentimes, we forget specific events, people and places that helped shape who we have become. Perhaps in reading the following accounts, you will find considerable delight.

A long time ago, we thought segregation should not be questioned. After all, that was our total experience at that time. This project allowed me to remember the bad, the good and the ugly and to review the earlier years in Bryan with a different lens. I came to understand (perhaps what many of us did not) that our parents were examples of the resilience embodied in an oppressed people. What they endured gave their children and neighbors the strength to overcome historical events, such as the establishment of the fugitive slave laws, the Civil War, the Dred Scott decision, black codes and obstacles that were set forth by the 1896 *Plessy v. Ferguson* "separate but equal" doctrine. Perhaps writing this book has afforded me an opportunity to see African American Bryan in a different context since its early years.

In searching recorded information, I found conflicting information in reference to dates, names and identification of individuals. For example, one source lists the date 1880 (ten years after Paul Laurence Dunbar, the first public school in Washington, D.C., was founded) as the date when twenty black students were enrolled in public school (according to the Brazos County Historical Time Line from 1880). In Sandra Farris's *History of Bryan*, Bryan Public School for Colored was founded in 1885, and its address was East Nineteenth Street, but the school was actually located between East Nineteenth and Twentieth Streets, near the corner of Houston Street. It's on Houston Street while its exits were on Twentieth Street, facing Preston Street.

The date given for the fire that destroyed the Washington Elementary School is also contradictory. According to Dr. Halcyon Sadberry

Watkins, the school was destroyed before Mr. Oliver Sadberry's death on December 4, 1970, not as previously believed. Yet another record of the birth date of Dr. William A. Hammond Sr. is 1898 instead of 1889.

When my classmates and I began first grade at Washington Elementary School, there were classrooms in four auxiliary frame buildings, three of which were located on East Nineteenth Street and one on North Preston Street. But according to G.F. Brundige, the brick building that replaced the 1914 frame building (Bryan Public School for Colored) was between East Nineteenth and Twentieth Streets, as aforementioned. The address given for E.A. Kemp Junior-Senior High School is West Nineteenth Street, but the school was actually located between West Twentieth and Twenty-first Streets, which were bordered by North Congress Street, where the school's entrances were located.

Wendell Davis is listed as one of the star players in the 1952–53 picture of E.A. Kemp's football team, but Wendell graduated in 1948. According to the same source, a 1966 track team picture features Merion Ellis, but the picture is labeled with the name Lawrence Ellis, who graduated in 1957. I tried to correct many of the inaccuracies by checking written records and official (legitimate) websites and by gathering information through interviews.

Historical facts, recollections and reflections of African Americans in Bryan, Texas, are presented in the pages that follow. It is my hope that readers of this history who still remember some parts of the time periods covered will travel down memory lane through each section with me and gain a new awareness and appreciation of times past without entirely forgetting the events and experiences they had in Bryan, Texas. Furthermore, I hope old wounds of invidious treatment, unequal opportunities and impoverished living conditions have faded deeply into the background of our collective memories.

HONOR AND RECOGNITION

So we stand here
On the edge of hell
In Harlem [Bryan]
And look out on the world
And wonder
What we're gonna do
In the face of
What we remember.
—Langston Hughes, "Harlem"

This book is written in honor and recognition of those who have suffered humiliations, insults and personal attacks because of their skin color. It is dedicated to the parents of Bryan's black students who bore the pain of wanting more for their children but did not have the means; who worked long days in the brutally hot Texas sun picking corn, cotton and onions in an effort to try to make ends meet. Fathers, especially those who were unskilled and had little education, were often not able to support their families and, as a result, turned to alcohol to dull their pain, which led to more humiliation and poverty. This book is for them, as well as the mothers who watched their sons go off to fight in wars for freedoms they did not enjoy; who did not have cars and, because Bryan did not have a public transit system, had to walk on sore, tired, aching feet to and from work every day; who worked in the homes of those who were well off while they themselves were paid as little as two dollars a day.

This book also honors those citizens who were not allowed to vote because they could not pay a poll tax and the young men who joined the armed forces to escape the social restrictions and circumstances that thwarted their ability to realize their potential and prevented them from succeeding.

This book is for all of these people and for all African Americans who, in spite of inadequate resources, strove for a better life for themselves and their families.

Langston Hughes's poem about Harlem at the beginning of this section is especially relevant and appropriate, as it personifies the feelings of many African Americans in Bryan, as well as African Americans throughout Brazos Valley, during hard times. In too many of the history books, African Americans have not been fully recognized for their many achievements and contributions. Perhaps this book is a good start toward highlighting and honoring their contributions and successes in face of incredible odds.

CHAPTER ONE
BACKGROUND AND HISTORY

In 2011, Mr. Oliver W. Sadberry Jr., curator of the Brazos Valley African American Museum, wrote an article entitled "Black Education in Brazos County." The following information is adapted from his article.

As the Brazos Valley was being settled in the 1840s, more and more slaves, skilled and unskilled, were brought in as laborers. Certain aspects of life, such as religious membership, marriage, property ownership and education, were denied to slaves. Most of them learned through oral history, trial and error and observation. On June 19, 1865, Texas slaves learned that they were free—two and a half years after the Emancipation Proclamation was signed on January 1, 1863. Today, African Americans in Texas commemorate and celebrate June 19 as the end of slavery in Texas.

Around the time of the slaves' emancipation in Texas, churches began to organize in the Brazos Valley, and marriage between slaves was recognized. The first formal institution that provided education for former slaves came about when a white man named W.W. Davis opened a school in 1865. The school had thirty-one females and thirty-nine males enrolled in its first year. Two other schools opened in Brazos County in 1866, one in Boonville, the first county seat of Brazos County, and the second in Millican. In 1871, the State of Texas passed the Public School Act. According to a website on the history of Bryan, Texas, Bryan was incorporated as a city in 1872 during the Reconstruction era. Bryan Independent School District (ISD) was established in 1877, but the first public school was not open until 1880, and it was for whites only. However, according to the Brazos County timeline, a

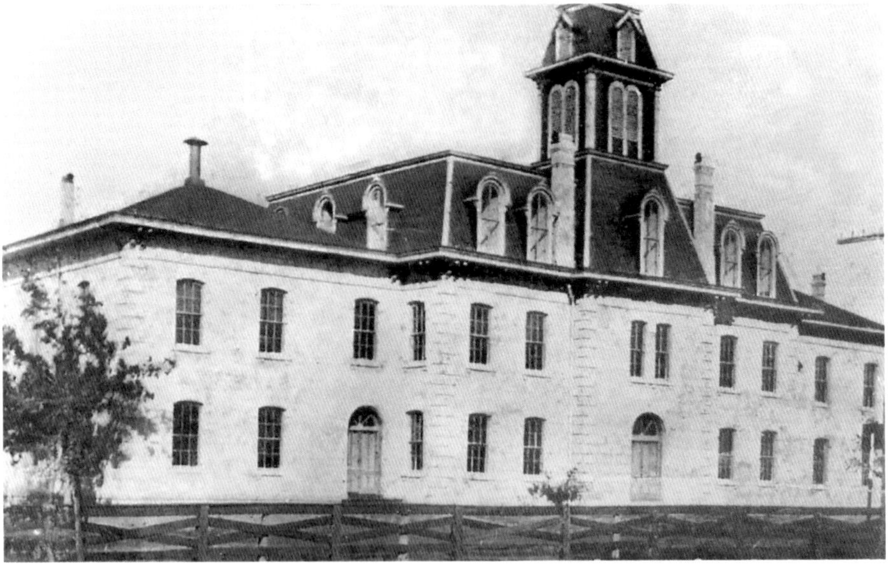

The first high school in Bryan was a three-story building built in 1880 for white students and was called Bryan High School. In 1929, the name was changed to Stephen F. Austin in honor of the Texas hero. Bryan schools were racially segregated until 1971. *Courtesy Carnegie Center of Brazos Valley History.*

school with twenty black students was also opened in October that year, and so, too, was a public school for black students. But according to Bryan ISD's records, the Bryan Public School for Colored opened in 1885, and that is the date used in this book.

Some historical background is important and necessary as a common reference point for understanding what living in African American Bryan was like. The term African American refers to race and is a proper noun. It replaces the word colored and other appellations used when referring to Negro citizens. The word colored was not, with few exceptions, capitalized, though it referred to race. In contrast, the word white, when referring to race, was almost always used as a proper noun and capitalized. Please note that the word from quoted documents in this book is expressed as it was at that time, although it is understood that black, colored and white are not proper nouns when referred to as race.

As aforementioned, the total time period of this project is from 1885 to 1971. Although the time period between 1971 and 2012 is covered, it is less emphasized. The time periods will be presented through historical facts, oral history, experiences, recollections and reflections, starting with Bryan Public

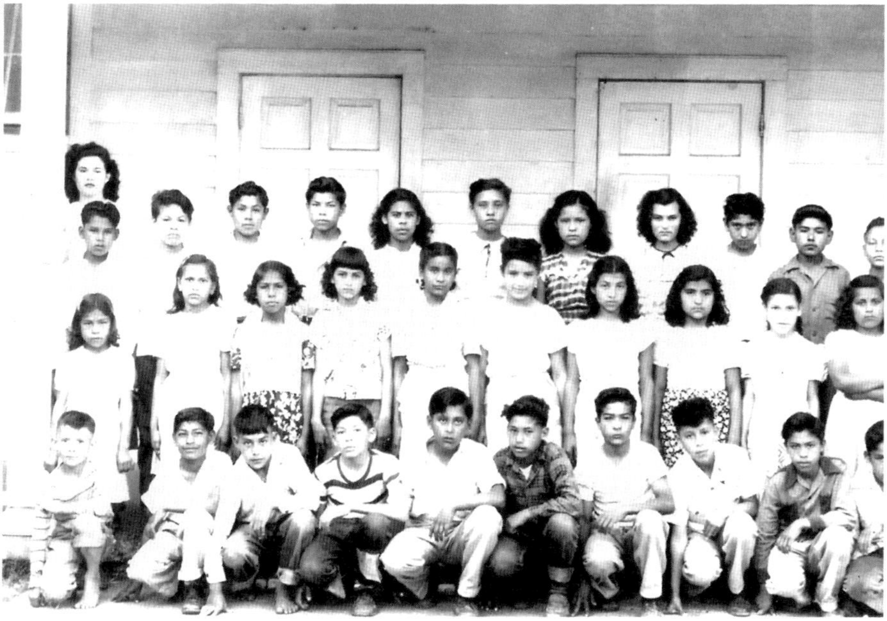

Ibarra School for Mexican Americans was the third racially segregated school in early Bryan. The actual date of the school's opening is not available. *Courtesy Carnegie Center of Brazos Valley History.*

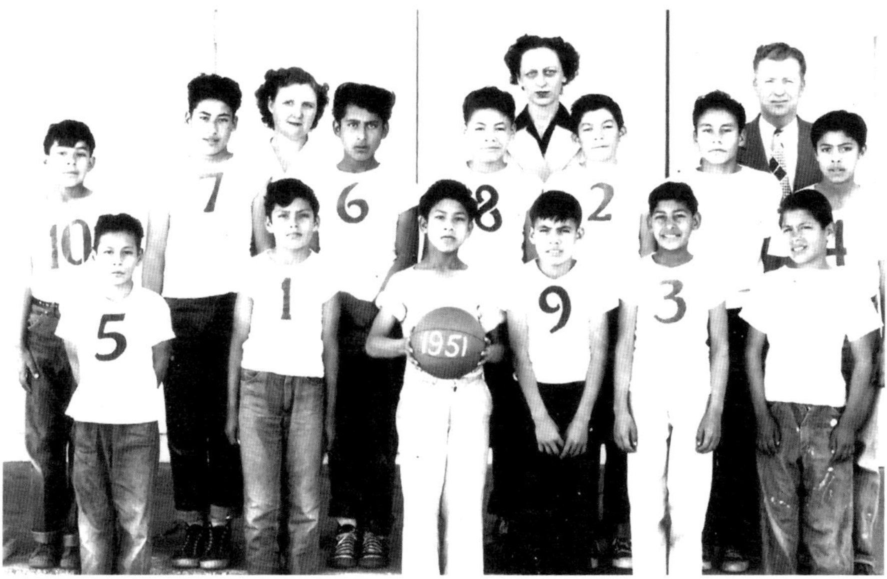

Students of the Ibarra School for Mexican Americans. *Courtesy Carnegie Center of Brazos Valley History.*

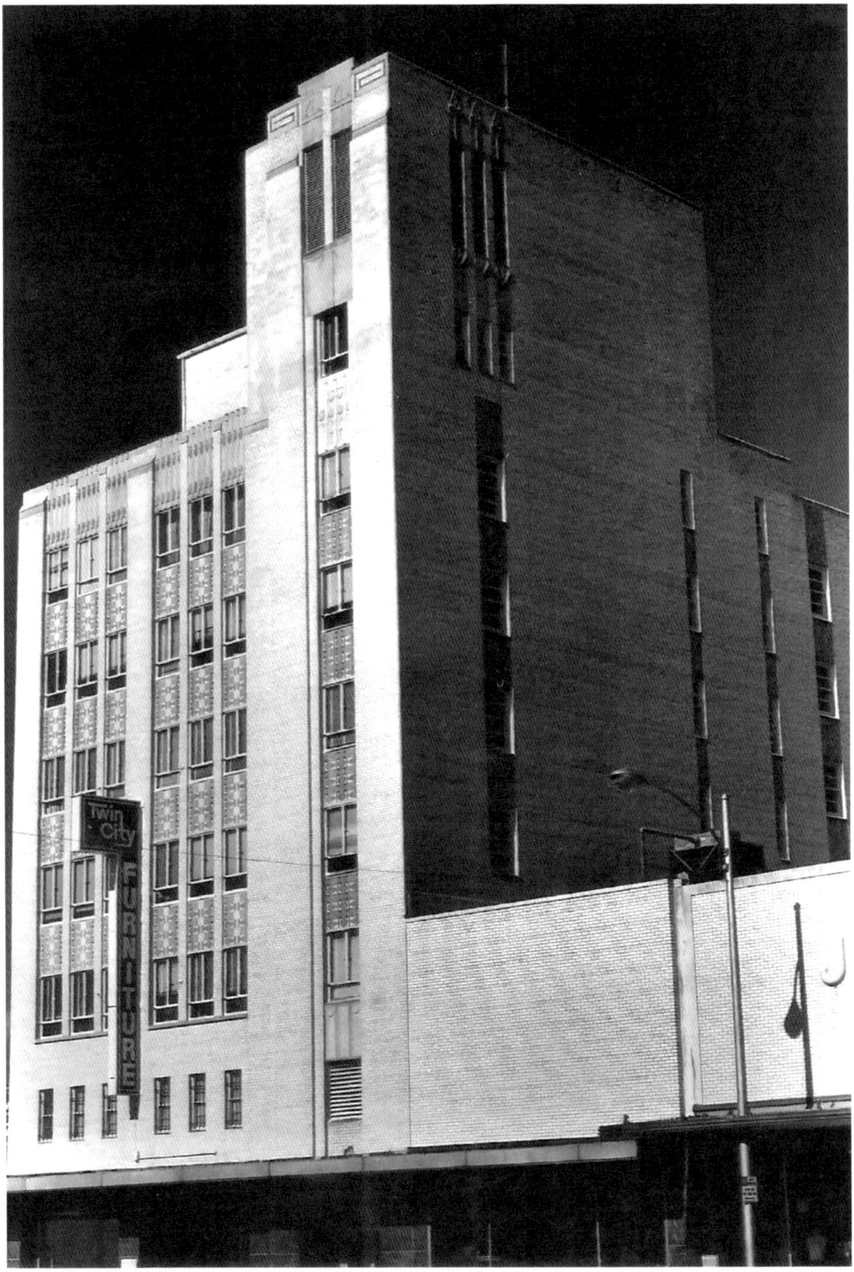

The Art Deco–style Varisco Building (circa 1949) at 219 North Street was considered Bryan's skyscraper. It was built by Brazos Varisco, one of the wealthiest Italian American businessmen in Brazos Valley. According to the *Bryan Daily Eagle*, Varisco died July 26, 1970, in Houston, Texas. *Courtesy Carnegie Center of Brazos Valley History.*

School for Colored, which was later named Washington Elementary School and was located between East Nineteenth and East Twentieth Streets, and E.A. Kemp Junior-Senior High School, originally located between Twentieth and Twenty-first Streets on the corner of North Congress Street.

Segregation in the Bryan ISD was ended when E.A. Kemp Senior High School and Stephen F. Austin were merged after immediate desegregation was ordered by the district court, as Farris records in her history of Bryan schools. Merging these two schools resulted in Bryan Senior High School, ending the long, contentious and stony road of school segregation. Prior to 1930, there was the Bryan Public School for whites, built in 1880, and Bryan Public School for Colored, built in 1885. According to the Handbook of Texas Online, this last school was established roughly nine years after the Texas State Constitution applied the "separate but equal" (though life would remain segregated and unequal) doctrine.

The Bryan Public School for Colored was a two-story frame structure that burned in 1914. It was replaced with the Washington Elementary School and was made of brick. While the new brick building was an improvement, the restrooms were not inside the building. Restrooms were later incorporated inside the building years later, along with new classrooms.

Bryan schools were segregated institutions in Brazos County from their beginnings, and the schools remained segregated until 1971, when they were finally integrated. To give the reader an idea of how segregated Bryan was at one time, there were three separate schools: one for African Americans, one for Mexican Americans (the Ibarra School) and one for whites. Although much of the discrimination Mexican Americans suffered was sanctioned more by custom than by statute, they were still not welcomed in many public accommodations. Many Italian Americans, who were considered white, lived in or owned businesses in the same neighborhoods as African Americans. In my youth, I thought it strange that their children did not attend the same schools with African Americans since they were in the same neighborhood. Some of the Italian Americans who lived or owned businesses in the neighborhoods were Jake Cangelosi, Charles Fererri, Niock Dalio, Don J. Fazzino, Mike Ferros (whose name I am not sure of, nor am I sure that he did indeed live in that neighborhood), Luke Graffizi, Tony Boatcallie, Johnny S. Lampo, Joe A. Restivo, Charles, John, Luke, Mike Ruffino and Frank Scalin.

The Ruffino name was popular among grocery store owners. Other Italian American surnames included the Palasotas, Scarmados and Variscos, especially Brazos Varisco, who built the Varisco Building, the tallest building in Bryan. The Varisco family is reportedly Bryan's first millionaire family.

FIRST GRADE: WASHINGTON ELEMENTARY SCHOOL TEACHERS

Before students enrolled in school, vaccinations were required. Boys and girls who lived on the town's east side received their immunization shots on Washington Elementary School's campus in a secondary frame building. These shots were required before entering the first grade. As aforementioned, the school did not have indoor plumbing, nor did it have a cafeteria, and students had to bring their lunches. For the most part, many students did not have lunch pails. Instead, they brought their lunches in brown paper bags. In fact, some students did not bring lunch at all because they were embarrassed at the fact that their parents (mine included) could not afford to buy a loaf of bread for sandwiches. I was lucky; my classmate Joe W. Toliver, a kid my grandmother used to babysit and a lifelong friend of mine, always shared his light bread (what loaf bread was called in those days) with me. Plus, his Aunt Bernice made hamburgers at the café on the corner of East Nineteenth Street near the school, and he often shared his hamburger with me. In Mrs. Doris Scurry's class, students had to identify and select food groups from magazines and tell classmates which foods they had for breakfast. Many times, we would say "ham and eggs" or "bacon and eggs," but the truth was that many of us had cornflakes with water and PET Milk. Oftentimes, some students had water and sugar, which was called "sweet water," or unpasteurized milk that came from Gertie M. Randle's mother's cows mixed with leftover cornbread. Some didn't eat breakfast at all.

When we began first grade, the following teachers were at Washington Elementary School: Anne Orabel Alberson, Irma Carter, Corine Cass, Lelia Hall, Eloise King, Juanita Martinez, Sylvia McIntosh, Lorraine Ocheltree, Doris Scurry and Mabel Thomas. Thomas Cole Sr. was the principal, and he later became the first dean and president of Wiley College. Teachers who joined the faculty while I was enrolled at Washington Elementary were Lula Callier, Ella Mae Gregg, Hattie Jackson, Vernell Jackson (no relation), Willie Pruitt, Geraldine Toliver and Jessie Mae Walton. Mr. Oliver Wayne Sadberry became principal after Thomas Cole Sr. The teachers, starting with the first grade and ending with the seventh, were Juanita Martinez, Sylvia McIntosh, Anne Orabel Alberson (who was erroneously listed as one of the first teachers at Bryan Public School for Colored), Doris Scurry, Lorraine Ocheltree, Irma Carter, Ella Mae Gregg and Lula Callier. Eloise King also joined the faculty as the music teacher.

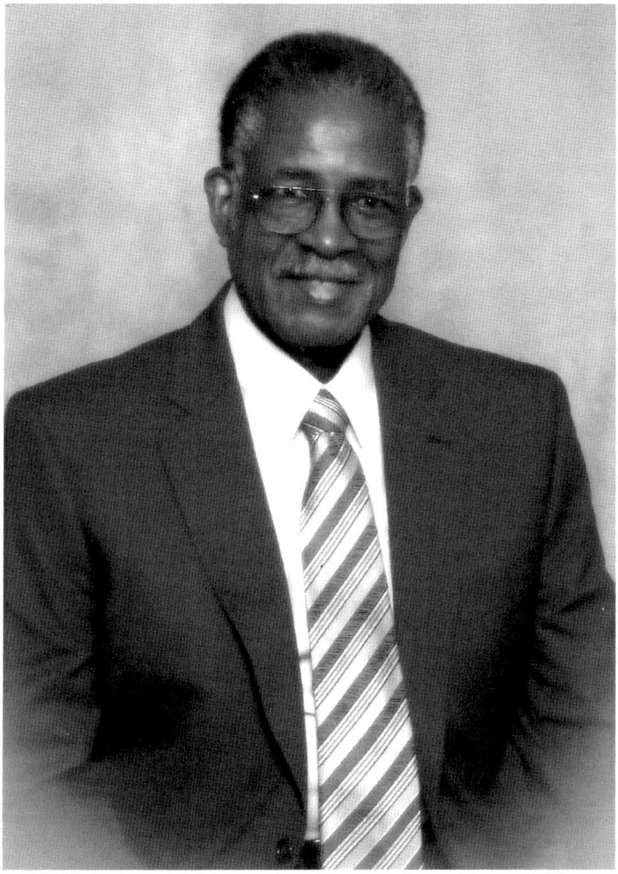

Leroy Sterling was the first African American to be officially admitted to Texas A&M University. He is also one of two African American E.A. Kemp alumni inducted in the Bryan ISD 2011 Hall of Honor. *Courtesy of Texas A&M University.*

To this day, I can still recall the first and last names of all my first-grade classmates except one. They are as follows: Willie Billy Alberson, Luther Baldwin, Luther Bauknite, Andrea Sue Carrol (Lucas), Jo Ann Cole, Homer C. Gillery, Sarah L. Greer Graham, Delores Jean Hall, Fred Hickman, Walter Peter Hollins, Ruben Terrell Jackson, Elmer Lindsay, Jessie Faye Ludd, Marvin (the one I can't remember!), William Mosely, Shelton "Pee Wee" Parker, Faye Thelma Patterson, Gloria Patton, Willie B. Perry, Otis Pierce, Robert Ross, Halcyon Sadberry, Opal Jean Sims, Joe W. Toliver, Jeanetta Walker and Melba Wilson. One classmate, Leroy Sterling, was the first African American to be officially enrolled at Texas A&M University, the first public university in Texas. He is also one of two African American E.A. Kemp alumni who were inducted into the first Bryan ISD Hall of Honor in 2011.

OTHER BRAZOS COUNTY SCHOOLS AND GEORGE WASHINGTON CARVER ELEMENTARY SCHOOL

There were other schools in Brazos County, such as Fairview and John M. Moore Vocational Training School, the latter of which was founded in 1941 and was the result of the consolidation of Dunbar, Prairie View Junior High School, Booker T. Washington Elementary, Cottonwood Elementary and Walker Settlement Elementary. According to Oliver Sadberry's article "Black Education in Brazos County," some of the teachers from the one-teacher schools that were consolidated were Blanche M. Berry, Annie B. Fennell, Annie Gray, Tenola Mosley and Pearline W. Stepp. The school name was changed to John M. Moore High School in 1943, and it was accredited. Principals of this school include: J.H. Coleman, Douglas Littleton, Fred Batts, Otha Byrd, Fannie Diggs, W.E. Stubblefield, Cluren Richardson and Wendell Davis, who was its last principal.

Some of the other earlier teachers at John M. Moore are listed below:

Olivia M. Banks
Thelma Buchanan±
William Cotton
Iney Cunningham±
Ella Donova
Mrs. A.M. Gray
Annette Green
Bama Hall±
Mae Edna Jones
Mable E. Knox
R.D. Littleton*
Albert Love
Walter McDaniel
Geraldine Powell
Annie D. Routt
Annie Simpson
R.L. Singletary
Edna Tarrow
B.J.H. Taylor Jr.
Veola Thomas
Lillian J. Walker
Lena Wilson

Other faculty of John M. Moore include:

Bus Drivers

Zubie Armstrong
James Bowser
Raymond Bowser
Albert Gaiter
Rev. P.C. Gray
Tobie Greer
Cecil Holston
James Lockridge
Clint Morrison
James Thurmond Ross
Henry Sillemon
Sylvester Teague
Emment Walton
Lee Wilson

Cafeteria Staff

Geneva Buchanan
Eula Johnson
Beatrice Toliver

*Served as a the school's principal (though some references list him as a superintendent)
±Former teacher at Fairview

John M. Moore burned down in 1949, reopened in 1952 and closed permanently in 1965.

In 1945, Washington was the only elementary school for African Americans in Bryan, so most of its students were from the west side. After 1949, children who lived on the west side attended George Washington Carver Elementary School. It was a brand-new school and was commonly referred to as Carver. All school-age children living on the west side were required to attend Carver. The friendships established with and among west side students while at Washington were rekindled a few years later in the eighth grade at E.A. Kemp Junior-Senior High School. However, according to Sadberry, the increase of rural schools resulted in thirty common school districts. These districts were eventually consolidated into three: Kurten (white), which is currently served by Bryan ISD; Fairview; and John M. Moore (both black).

Some of the principals at Fairview were Fred D. Batts, Theodore Brown, Fannie Diggs, John T. Lane and Oliver W. Sadberry Sr. Teachers at Carver included Roosevelt Brown, Inez Cunningham, Sally Jane Austin, Chanie Dix, Pauline Hatchett and Eula Cunningham. The districts were incorporated into Bryan ISD and A&M Consolidated Independent School District in 1928. African American students living in this district were taught at elementary and junior high school level in the communities of College Hills, Dowling, Peach Creek, Providence, Shirock, Sulphur Springs, Union Hills, Washington Chapel and Wellborn. However, African American high school students from College Station attended E.A. Kemp Junior-Senior in Bryan until College Station's A&M Consolidated Negro School was built in 1941. The first principal was Elbert Cunningham, and teachers at the school included Thay Myrtle Owens, Edna Harris and Willie Tarrow (residents of Bryan), A.J. Thompson, Ruth Cunningham and James Hawkins. The school changed its name to Lincoln High in 1946. That same year, W.D.

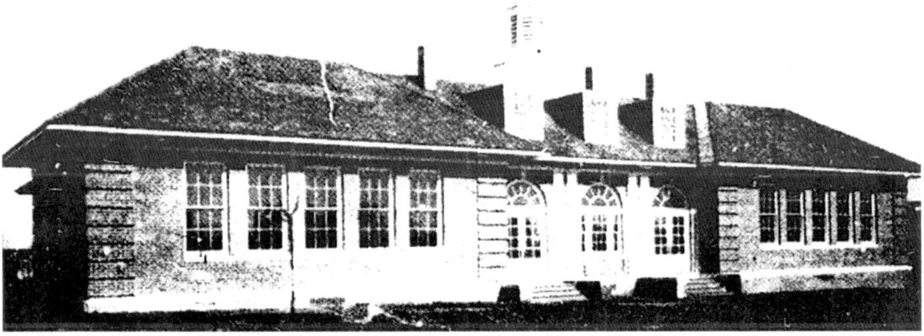

Washington Elementary School replaced the Bryan Public School for Colored after it burned down in 1914. *Courtesy Carnegie Center of Brazos Valley History.*

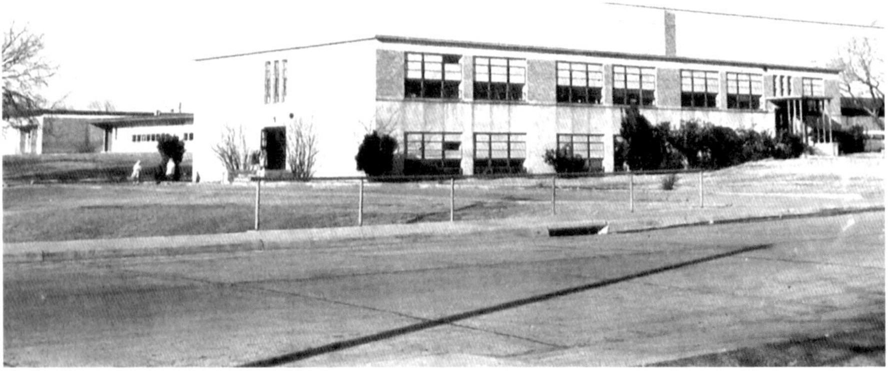

George Washington Carver Elementary School was built in 1949 on Bryan's west side and was the second elementary school for black students. Students who lived on the west side no longer had to walk the distance to Washington Elementary School, which was previously the only local elementary school. The school's first principal was Mr. Colquitt D. Yancy. *Courtesy Dr. Adolph Johnson Jr.*

Bunting, a white man, was appointed superintendent of the Brazos County District, and Willie A. Tarrow of Bryan was named principal of Lincoln High School.

In 1949, Mr. Oliver Wayne Sadberry Sr. became principal of Washington Elementary School. He provided excellent leadership for faculty members, students and the Bryan community for over twenty years. In fact, his influence was profoundly felt, as he was not only a teacher and a principal but also a mentor and friend. I can still hear him saying, "Oswell, the world

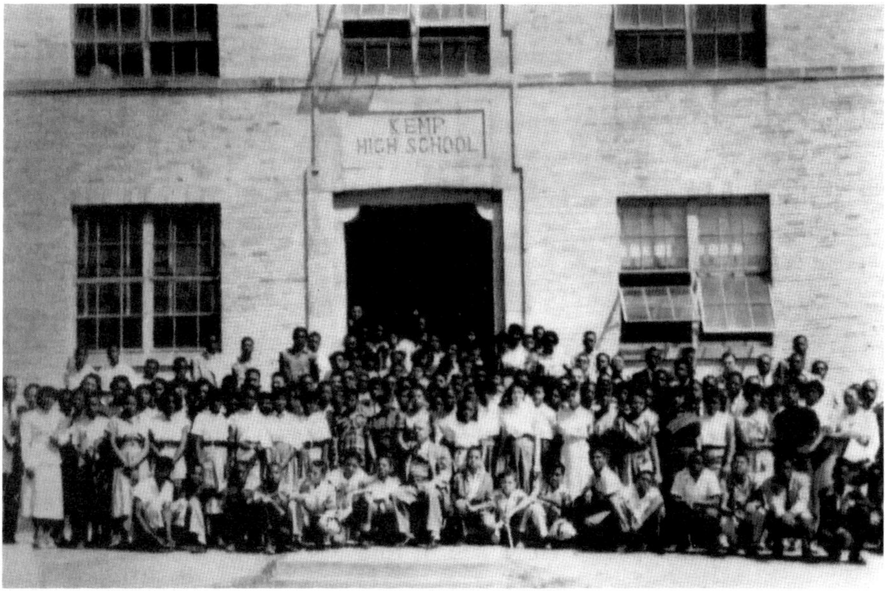

E.A. Kemp Junior-Senior High School, commonly referred to as Kemp, was built in 1930 and was named after Elijah Alonzo Kemp, the African American principal of Bryan Public School for Colored. *Courtesy Carnegie Center of Bryan Valley History.*

needs finely trained men and women." It seemed like an odd expression at the time, but he was trying to prepare us for a future we could not imagine. Another saying of his was "Boys and girls, don't be mediocre." The last letter I received from him was in 1969, when he wrote to me and offered me a teaching job at Washington. Unfortunately, I could not accept his invitation because I was about to start graduate school.

As previously mentioned, Bryan Public School for Colored was replaced by Washington Elementary School after a new school was built on the west side in 1930. The new school was E.A. Kemp Junior-Senior High School, named after Elijah Alonzo Kemp, one of the early African American principals of Bryan Public School for Colored.

In 1929, the Bryan School ISD renamed Bryan High School for whites after a Texas hero named Stephen F. Austin. By 1939, the student population at Stephen F. Austin High had increased so much that a new and larger school was needed. According to the History of Bryan ISD, the new Stephen F. Austin High School was built at 801 South Ennis Street and remained at that location until a U.S. district court ordered immediate desegregation in 1971. Following that court order, it became a junior high

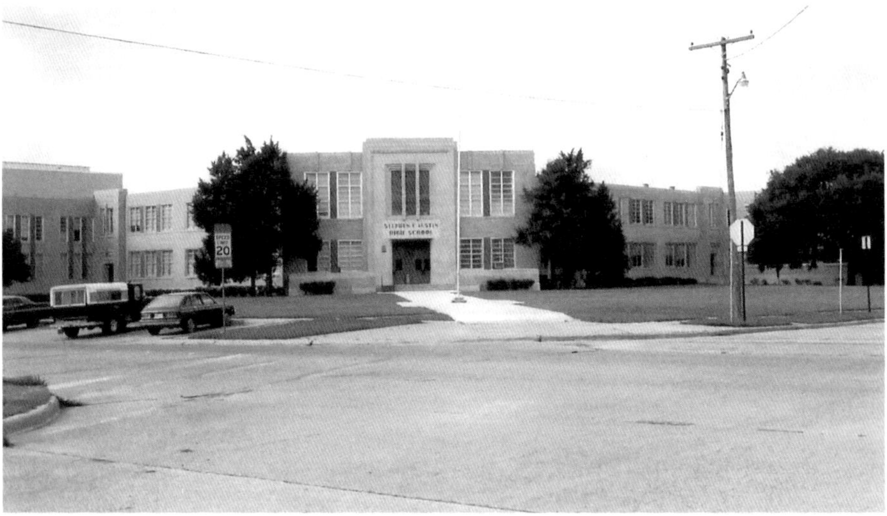

Bryan Public School, which was for white students only, was renamed Stephen F. Austin in honor of the Texas hero. This picture is of the new Stephen F. Austin School on Ennis Street, where the school remained until the court-ordered immediate desegregation in 1971. *Courtesy Carnegie Center of Brazos Valley History.*

school. According to Anne Boykin's article "College Station, Texas: A City on the Right Track," the desegregation order came five years after schools in the neighboring College Station ISD, including Lincoln High, the school for African Americans, were desegregated.

E.A. KEMP JUNIOR-SENIOR HIGH SCHOOL

The newly named E.A. Kemp Junior-Senior High School, built in 1930, was reported to have been quite modern, although it did not have a gymnasium or cafeteria. The gymnasium that was built later was a tin, barn-like structure that was equipped with industrial fans instead of air conditioning. It did, however, provide showers for athletes and physical education students. As I recall, no cafeteria was ever added to the 1930 facility.

The faculty at the time my classmates and I attended E.A. Kemp Junior-Senior High School were

Louise Anderson
Robert Guyden
James Johnson
Willa Johnson
Willie Moore
A.K. O'Neal
Mel Pruitt
Claude L. Scurry
Sadie Thomas
Mr. Webster
Waymon Webster
Johnnie P. Wyatt

Both Mr. Webster and Mr. Johnson earned their PhDs and served as university administrators at Prairie View A&M University and Texas Southern University, respectively. Robert Claudius Neal (known as R.C. Neal) was the school's principal, and Sylvia Sadberry was the school secretary. Some of the others who joined the faculty later were Betty J. Hatchett, Marion Haynes, Edessie McClendon, Hiawatha Webber, Freddie M. Martin Robinson, Bernice Webster, Olivia Banks and Colquitt D. Yancy, who became principal when R.C. Neal retired.

Although the new E.A. Kemp Junior-Senior High School did not have a cafeteria, students and faculty had six places where they could eat. Scott's Diner was just across the street, and many students and faculty members enjoyed hot lunches there. Campus Inn was also across the street, near the corner of North Congress Street, and it served up hot dogs, hamburgers, chips and sodas. Littleton's Snack Bar was a third choice for fast-food, such as hot dogs, hamburgers, floats and French fries. I'll note here that Washington Elementary School, like E.A. Kemp Junior-Senior High, did not have a cafeteria when I started. But Mr. Stearne, who owned a grocery store near the campus, let students who would have otherwise gone without buy lunchmeat, saltines and sodas for ten to fifteen cents. Many other stores adopted this same practice. Sam Mosely's grocery store, which was across the street from Littleton's Snack Bar, was another lunch spot. There, students could buy lunchmeat, saltines, chips and sodas for ten to twenty cents. The fifth choice for lunch was Nelson's café, called the Blue Dine Inn, which was on the same block. The last place was Scanlin's grocery store, located at the corner of West Nineteenth and North Congress Streets.

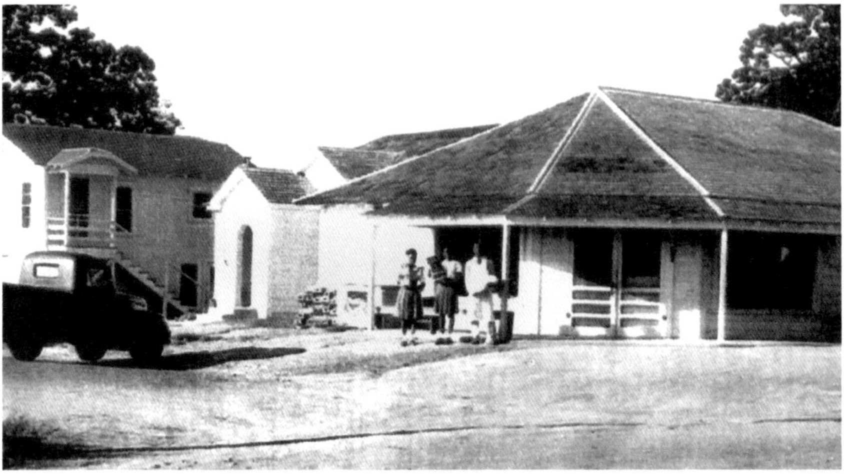

This picture of Sam Mosely's grocery store was taken in the 1940s. Here, Mr. Mosely is standing in front of the store with two young female relatives, Ethel and Lula Whitfield. Mosely may have been the only African American grocer who provided such service. The store was attached to living quarters, which was common at that time. *Courtesy of daughter Barbara Faye Mosely.*

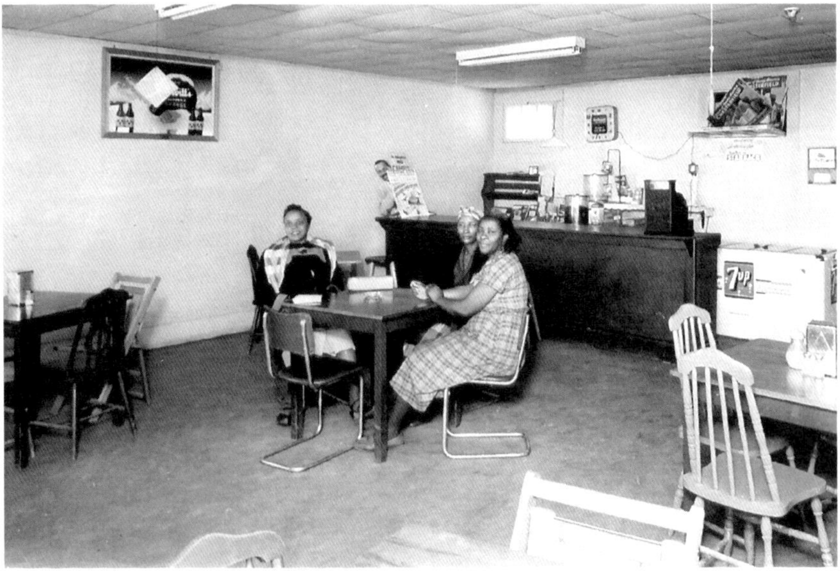

The Blue Dine Inn was established in the early 1950s on West Nineteenth Street and was operated by Mr. and Mrs. Horace Nelson Sr. It was one of several eateries where E.A. Kemp students and faculty could get a hot meal during the school day. It was also a safe place where youth could congregate and socialize on the weekends. Mrs. Nelson is seated on the right with two other females. *Courtesy of Charles Nelson.*

E.A. Kemp Senior High School and R.C. Neal Junior High School

By 1960, Bryan's population had reached over 27,542, and this increase in population created the need for a new high school for African Americans. As a result, E.A. Senior High School was built at 1601 West Nineteenth Street. Unlike the junior-senior high school, the new school had a cafeteria and gymnasium. It was the first school that senior high students did not share with junior high students. Upon completion of E.A. Kemp Senior High, Bryan had four schools for African Americans. After the high school was built, the former E.A. Kemp Junior-Senior High School was renamed R.C. Neal Junior High. The school was run by three principals over its nine-year existence: Ulysses S. Morgan, Dr. Wendell Davis Jr. (who was a former student, football player and track and field star) and Claude L. Scurry, legendary coach for the E.A. Kemp Bears. Sadly, the school was destroyed by fire, but the treasured memories live on. In spite of segregation as a way of life, many African Americans made noteworthy contributions to our community, many of whom were small business owners, professionals, civic leaders, educators and parents.

E.A. Kemp High Extracurricular Activities

Boys at E.A. Kemp High School could participate in all three sports—basketball, football and track and field; girls participated in basketball and track and field. The school's mascot was a bear, but the athletes played like tigers against competitors in football. The players demonstrated the heroic courage and tenacity in sports that was exemplified by the African American community in general.

Although Kemp was small, it competed against big-city teams, including Austin, Beaumont, Corpus Christi, Galveston, Port Arthur, San Antonio and Waco. The school also played against small city teams in Calvert, Corsicana, Hearne, Hillsboro, Marlin, Mexia, Temple and Tyler. The Anderson High Yellow Jackets (Austin) were stiff competition and had the distinction of having the largest marching band in the conference. Carver High (Waco), Central High (Galveston), Herbert (Beaumont), Lincoln High (Port Arthur), Phyllis Wheatley (San Antonio) and Solomon Cole (Corpus Christi) were schools, as expected, with superior teams. But for the most part, the Bears usually fared well in football against the big-city teams and were generally superior against smaller teams.

The roster of football players consisted of outstanding and exceptional athletes, and some even lettered in all three varsity sports. Players like Bruce Barrow, William Cavitt, William Hall, Wesley Hannah, Jethro Hatchett, Dixon McIntosh, Kermit Scott and Finnis Williams filled out the roster at Bryan Public School for Colored, E.A. Kemp Junior-Senior's predecessor. Dixon McIntosh's wife, Sylvia, was my second-grade teacher, and Kermit Scott was a relative of Hollywood personality Bob Scott, known for his role in the 1948 movie *Look Out Sister*.

Some of the football (FT) players in the 1940s who lettered in one or all three of E.A. Kemp's sports were:

Arthur Adams (FT)
Bill Albright (FT)
Jody Banks (FT)
James Boone (FT)
Ralph Campbell (FT)
Sloan Clopton (FT)
Edward L. Colquitt (FT)
Wendell Davis (B-FT-TF)
Robert Graves (FT)
Robert Green (FT)
Clifton Greer (FT)
James (Jim) Greer (FT)
Marion Haynes (FT)
James Hill (FT)
Romalis Lane (FT)
Walter Patton (FT)
Felix Petty (FT)
Charlie Sanders (FT)
Joe Willie Toliver (FT)
Hiawatha Webber (FT)
Otha White (FT)
Collie Williams (FT)
Marion "Buck" Williams (FT)

Clifton Greer moved to San Francisco in 1945, where he still resides, and his brother, James Greer, lives in Oakland, California. Dr. Wendell Davis, who was the captain of the 1948 squad, died in September 2009. Wendell Davis was also an exceptional track star who set an unbroken record for running the fastest 100 meters and participated in the Olympic trials. Edward L. Colquitt, who was Davis's co-captain, currently lives in Richmond, California. Joe Willie Toliver served as a captain on Seattle's police force and has recently retired. Marion "Buck" Williams lived in New York for a number of years but came back to Bryan, where he operated a barbershop. He died in 2011.

The teams between the years 1950 to 1959 continued to shine on the football field, as well as in other sports.

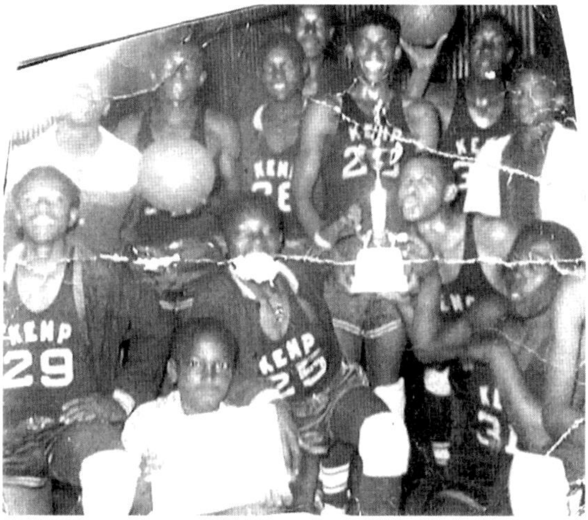

E.A. Kemp basketball players for the 1953–54 season. The team was the runner-up in the state championship that year. *Front*: Trainer Luther Baldwin. *Second row kneeling, from left to right*: Lloyd Walker, Harrell Johnson, Melvin Turner and unknown student. *Third row, standing, from left to right*: John Dunn, Robert Smith, William Dunn, George Vaults and Billy R. Smith. The first player in the back is not recognized, and Clifton Holland is holding the basketball. *Courtesy George Vaults.*

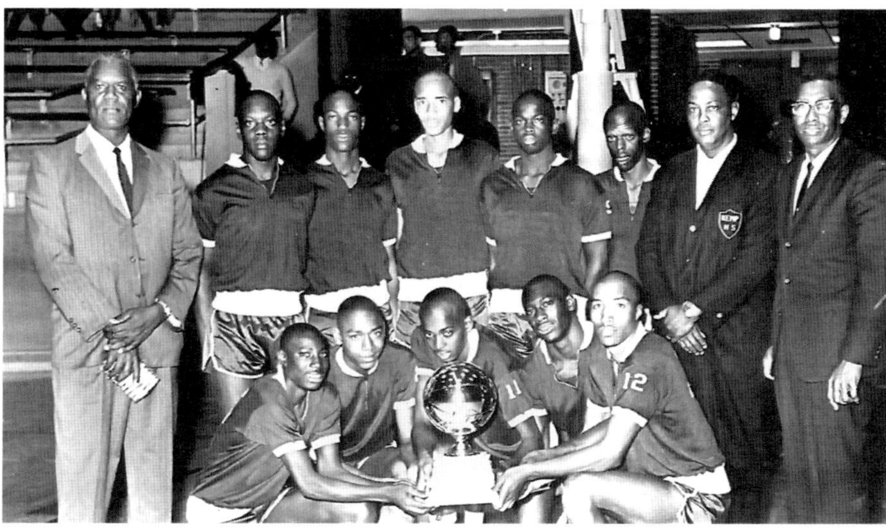

E.A. Kemp Senior High basketball players for the 1965–66 team. The team was runner-up in the state championship that year. *Keeling in first row, left to right*: Horace Jones, Arthur Sandle, James Bailey, Captain Johnny Williams and Robert Thornton, co-captain. *Standing, left to right*: Coach Claude L. Scurry, Otis Asberry, Billy Amerson, Benjamin Nicks, Otis Carter, James Nixon, Assistant Coach Robert Guyden and Principal W.D. Dunn. *Courtesy Dr. Adolph Johnson Jr.*

Novella Gafford
Emmaline Gause
Nettie Heads
Erma Faye Hedge
Robbie Hill
Shirley Holland
Margie Holloway
Mildred Hughes
Shirley Knox
Anne R. Johnson
Dorothy Lewis
Rudell Moore
Pearl Ester Murkledove
Mary C. Myers
Sandra L. Nicks
Annette Norwood
Lilly Norwood
Mary L. Norwood
Carolyn Peterson
Barbara Richardson
Mary A. Smith
Nettie E. Thurman
Mildred Tramble+
Mineola Vaults
Earnestine Wilson

Although all the girls were good, the ones with plus signs by their names were rated outstanding.

As far as I can remember, Billie J. Turner and Doris Green were the standout runners for the girls' track and field teams from 1952 to 1956. The boys' track and field teams were just as good as, if not better than, many of the competing schools. Some of the outstanding members were Marion Haynes and Johnny Ellis, both of whom still live in Bryan; Clarence "Bo" Stephney (deceased); Isaac "Long John" Watson; and Roger Turner, who retired from the U.S. Army and now lives in Lawton, Oklahoma. Johnny Ellis and Marion Haynes ran the 100 meters, while the last three were long-distance runners.

Baseball was later added as a team sport. Horace Jones, Roland Koontz, Leon Murphy, Benjamin Nicks, Robert Person, Ernest Scott and Charles Williams played on the team in its early years. Here's a list of some other talented players in all sports who received athletic scholarships between the years 1948 and 1960:

Sloan Clopton
Edward L. Colquitt
Wendell Davis
Robert Ellis
Elmaurice Harris
Marion Haynes
Clifton Holland
Frank Perry
Lorenzo Scurry
Joe Willie Toliver
Tommy Traylor
George Vaults
John L. Williams
Lloyd Williams
Marion Williams

Tommy Traylor was an outstanding quarterback who ran a kickoff return the length of the football field against Dallas's Booker T. Washington High School team. Bobby Hill was arguably the best basketball player in Brazos County's memory. William G. Hall currently lives in Calvert, Texas. Joe Perry currently lives in Bryan.

In addition to athletics, E.A. Kemp had a marching band, a cheerleading squad, a drill team, majorettes and an outstanding choir. The band and cheerleaders provided moral support and encouraged the teams to victory, promoting school spirit, pride and unity. Some members of the band, choir, cheerleaders, drill teams and majorettes are listed here:

E.A. Kemp Marching Band

James Alberson
Irene Bradle
Herman O. Brown
Coakey E. Carroll
Donald Childs
Leon Davis
Nathaniel Dove
Etta Duren
Ennis Green
Albert Griffin
Fred Hickman
Clifton Holland
Shirley Holland
Donald Ray Johnson
Floyd Johnson
Marion Jones
Joyce King
Edward H. Knox Jr.
John J. Knox
Sylvester Lewis
Melvin Littleton
Oscar Lee Morgan
Lonnie Mulkey
James T. Murphy

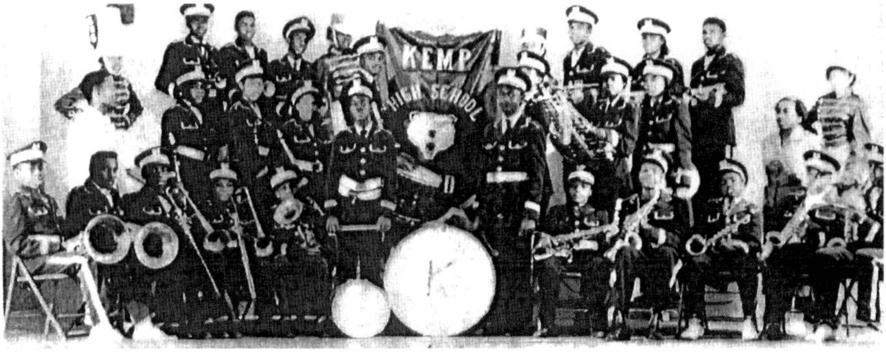

E.A. Kemp band in the early 1950s. *Front row, seated, left to right*: David Hollins, Joe W. Toliver, Willie Taylor, Rachel Jackson and an unknown student; *standing*: Horace Nelson and Rozell Quarles; *seated*: Marion Jones, Charles Pharms, James H. Alberson, Edward Knox, Melvin Littleton. *Second row, standing, left to right*: Mr. Waymon Webster, band director Etta Duren, Joyce King, Janice Thurman, Ennis Green, unknown student, Iona Richardson, Alice J. Tyler, unknown student and Mrs. Mel Pruitt. *Top row, standing, left to right*: Unknown, Fred Hickman, James Turner, Nat Dove, Dorothy J. Banks, Erma J. Hawkins, Floyd Johnson, Darlene Sheppard, Sidney E. Simpson and Eva Lois Harrison. *Courtesy Carnegie Center of Brazos Valley History.*

Horace Nelson
Charles Pharms
Rozell Quarle
Ina Richardson
Collie Sanders
Lorenzo Scurry
Robert J. Shields
Juree Shivers
Sidney Simpson
Billy R. Smith
Fred G. Smith
Mazie Nell Smith
Samuel Smith
William Smith
Willie C. Smith
Janice Thurman
Jimmy L. Tillery
Joe W. Tolive
James Turner
Alyce Tyler
Billy Walker
Weldon Walton
Charles Watson
Jurline Wilson

A Cappella Choir

Billy Alberson
Luther Baldwin
Rastine Calhoun
Samuel Callier
Etta Duren
Charles E. Ellis
Bessie Gibbs
Dorothy Green
Gladys Green
Georgia Kennard
Gloria Knox
Ina Richardson
Lorenzo Scurry
Darlene Sheppard
Opel Sims
Willie C. Smith
Walter Sterling
John D. White
Cloyd Williams
John L. Williams

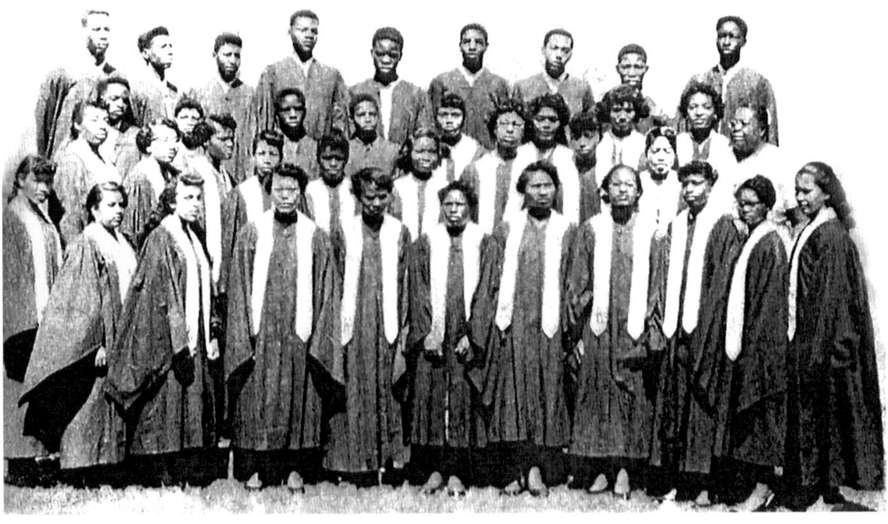

In addition to having talented athletes, E.A. Kemp had several a cappella choirs that were under the inimitable direction of Mrs. Johnnie P. Wyatt, a graduate of Bryan Public School for Colored. Students in the choir had exceptional musical talent and great voices. One of Mrs. Wyatt's students even went on to attend Juilliard School of Music. *Courtesy Carnegie Center of Brazos Valley History.*

Cheerleaders

Sandra Alexander
Patricia Brown
Lela Burton
Emmaline Gause
Erma F. Goffney
Doris Green
Ruby L. Green
Margie Holloway
Annie R. Johnson
Ruby Newton
Frank Perry
Mildred Ray
Joan Robertson
Lorenza Shirley
Sheryl Shivers
Clarence Stephen
Alyce Tyler
Laura J. Ward

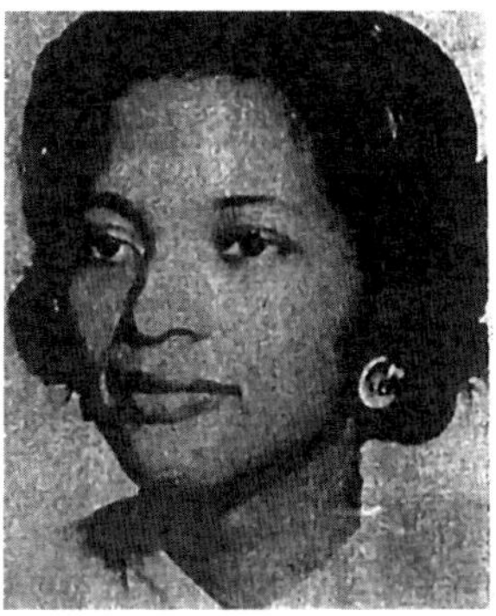
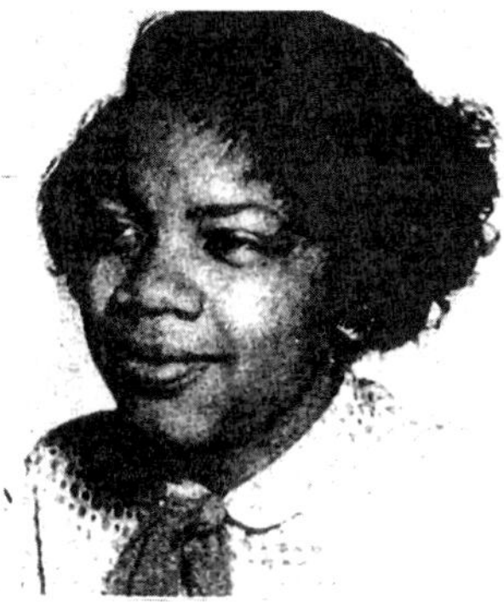
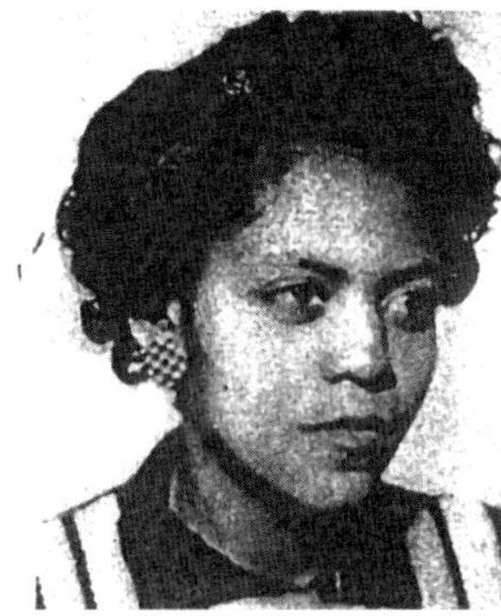

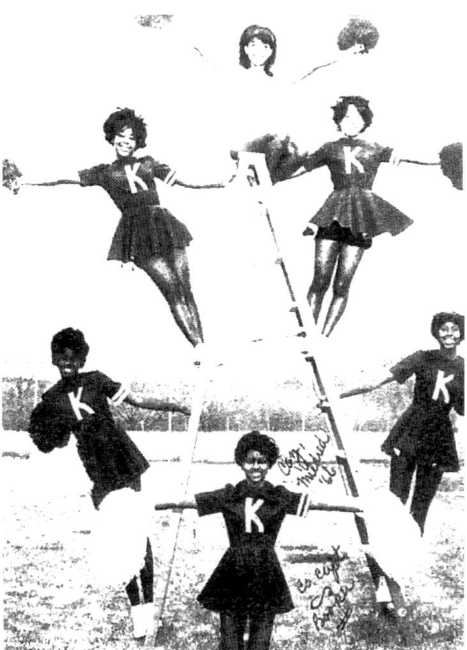

Above: E.A. Kemp cheerleaders played an invaluable role in promoting school pride, spirit and unity. Pictured here are three cheerleaders from the class of 1955. *From left to right:* Lela Burton, Erma Faye Goffney and Ruby Lois Green (who was also on the drill squad). *Courtesy Carnegie Center of Brazos Valley History.*

Left: E.A. Kemp cheerleaders from the class of 1966. Mildred Ray (bottom) and Joan Robertson are on the left. Patricia Brown (bottom) and Sandra Alexander are on the right. Ruby Newton is the center and Sheryl Shivers is on top. *Courtesy Dr. Adolph Johnson Jr.*

Drill Squad

Amy L. Bradley
Erma Goffney
Ruby Green
Lanetta Hollins
Mary A. Lewis
Johnnie Patterson
Iona Potts
Ina Richardson

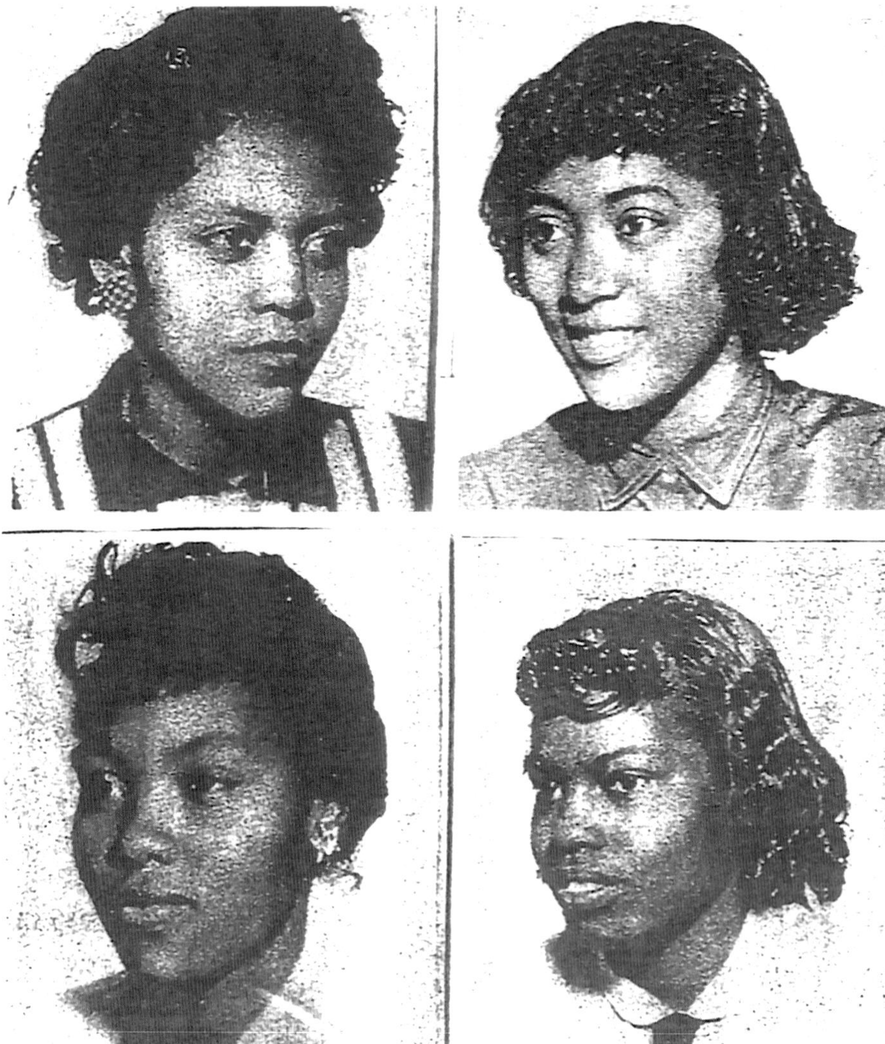

E.A. Kemp drill squad from the class of 1955. *At bottom, from left to right*: Iona Potts and Ina Richardson. *At top, left to right*: Ruby Lois Green and Johnnie Patterson. *Courtesy Carnegie Center of Brazos Valley History.*

Majorettes

Dorothy J. Banks
Irene Bradley
Barbara R. Calhoun
Shirley Chambers
Charlie M. Davis
Doris J. Ford
Bessie Gibbs
Eva Lois Harrison
Erma J. Hawkins
Peggy Humphrey
Georgia Johnson
Carolynne King
Doris Mcrae
Melba Moore
Maxine Morris
Blossie T. Philips
Gladys Sanders
Darlene Sheppard
Jo Floy Shirley
Tina B. Sims
Gwendolyn Stearne
Lorraine Sterling
Melvin Taylor
Doris Thompson
Georgia Tramble
Melvin Jean Traylor
Ray Watson
Era Whitehead

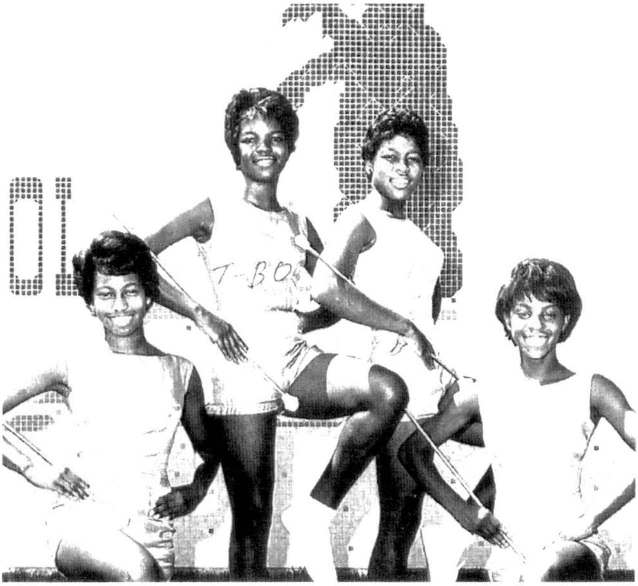

Pictured here are E.A. Kemp majorettes from the classes of 1967 (kneeling) and 1968 (standing). *Standing, from left to right*: Melvin Taylor and Era Whitehead. *Kneeling, from left to right*: Melba Moore and Doris Thompson. *Courtesy Carnegie Center of Brazos Valley History and Dr. Adolph Johnson Jr.*

There were other clubs and organizations that gave students a chance to demonstrate their abilities and talents: Dramatic Arts Club, Hi-Y Club, Jets Club, Leadership Club, Lettermen's Club, Jazz Band and Tri-Y Club. Two of the several student organizations included the student council and the National Honor Society. Adolph Johnson Jr., Mildred Ray, Linda Smith and Marva Wilson were charter members of the National Honor Society.

Performing Arts: Jazz and Blues Bands

E.A. Kemp had many talented student musicians. In the 1950s and '60s, the student musicians came under the influence and tutelage of band directors Hardy Ray Murphy, Dr. Waymon Webster, A.C. Shead and, at some point, William D. Portis. Of these band directors, Dr. Waymon Webster had the greatest impact on the aspirations and careers of the up-and-coming young musicians. Dr. Webster was more than the typical band director: he helped his students see into the future by raising their horizons beyond Bryan. Furthermore, he set himself apart from other band directors by teaching music harmony, theory, conducting, orchestration and music arranging. One of his former students, Nathaniel Dove, paid special honor to Dr. Webster, presenting him with the Bakersfield Blues Preservation Society Plaque in 2006. Some of the young students whose musical talent was nurtured by Dr. Webster, affectionately known by students as Jack, and who went on to become professional musicians were Fred G. Smith, Lorenzo "Bunny" Scurry, Nathaniel "Nat" Dove, Marion "Boddie" Jones, Donald "Dickie" Childs, Albert Griffin, Donald Ray Johnson and Clyde Dove, Nat's brother.

Many of these musicians further honed their skills in local night spots in Bryan and other venues in Texas. Some left Bryan and played in cities and states like Albuquerque, New Mexico; Las Vegas, Nevada; and Los Angeles and San Francisco, California. Here is a small list of musicians who played in venues in the United States only:

Donald "Dickie" Childs, a saxophonist, played in clubs and other venues in Texas and attended the University of North Texas (formerly North Texas State).

Clyde Dove played blues music on the piano in and around Bryan before leaving for California. Since moving to California, he has switched his talents to gospel music. Clyde currently resides in Inglewood, California.

Albert Griffin, as he was known at E.A. Kemp, is a pianist. He is proficient in blues, classical and Top-Forty, but as he will tell you, "Jazz is his bread and butter." Albert now goes by Damu Sudi Ali and has been a regular at the Lazy Lees Jazz Bistro in San Francisco for the past eight years. His latest CD, *Dance of the Kalahari*, is "red hot." He also has a CD of original compositions and is soon to release a new album with his son, Jabari Ali. Damu also played with the Umoja Band, attended Texas A&M University and Laney College and now teaches music at a private middle school in Oakland, California.

Marion "Boddie" Jones was a tremendously gifted saxophonist from E.A. Kemp who attended the University of North Texas, where he was a member of one of the renowned Jazz Lab bands. He too played the night spots in and around Bryan and other venues in Texas before relocating to Los Angeles, where he became a Hollywood studio musician. Lorenzo "Bunny" Scurry was arguably the best trumpet player ever to come out of E.A. Kemp. He was a regular in nightclubs in Las Vegas for many years.

Still, a few E.A. Kemp alumni lived and played in Belgium; Canada; Paris, France; and Tokyo, Japan. Fred G. Smith was another very gifted saxophonist (according to his teacher) with perfect pitch. As a high school student, his sounds were comparable to the likes of Charlie Byrd, Paul Desmond, Dexter Gordon and Sonny Rollins. Fred played in nightclubs in Bryan and other cities throughout Texas. He attended the University of Texas's and the University of North Texas's graduate schools for music. Fred formed a Fred Gene Combo while attending graduate school at the University of Texas and played many of Texas's big cities before moving to California in 1969. Fred also wrote and arranged music for Smokey Robinson. In fact, he wrote "Quiet Storm" while with the legendary Smokey Robinson's group. He played with the late Ray Charles's orchestra and toured in the United States, as well as other countries.

Donald Ray Johnson is a gifted blues drummer and vocalist who was influenced by Dr. Webster to pursue a career in music. He played in various concert halls across the States, as well as jazz festivals in Belgium, Canada, France and Switzerland. Donald is an international recording artist and released albums in 1998, 2002 and 2006. I had the pleasure of both meeting and talking via telephone with Donald while he was playing a jazz festival in France on March 24, 2010. Donald won a Grammy in 1979 while playing with a group called the Taste of Honey. He was voted best male blues vocalist in 2007 by *Real Blues Magazine* and won the 2008 Blewzzy Award. Donald's

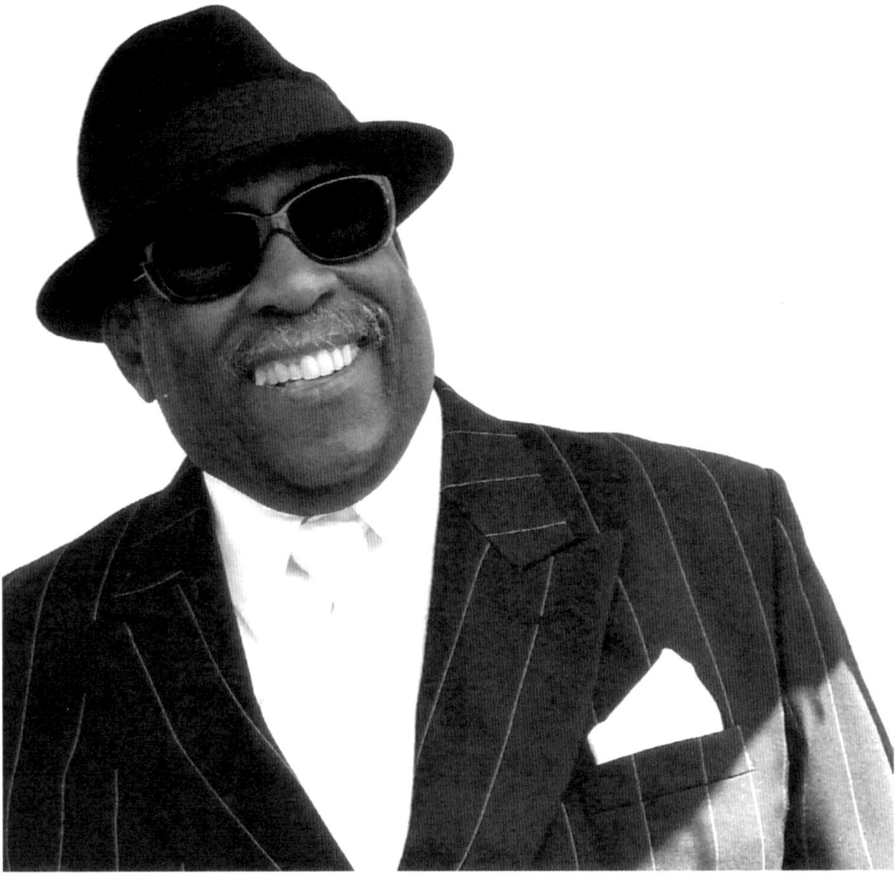

Donald Ray Johnson is a gifted blues drummer and vocalist who was influenced to pursue a career in music by Dr. Waymon T. Webster and Mr. William Portis, both of whom were band directors at E.A. Kemp High from 1952 to 1963 and 1968 to 1971, respectively. Johnson has played in concert halls and jazz festivals in America, Belgium, Canada, France and Switzerland. *Courtesy Donald Ray Johnson.*

many credits and musical contributions are listed on his website at www.donaldrayjohnson.com. Donald is based in Calgary, Canada, where he has lived for over twenty years, and he holds dual citizenship in Canada and the United States.

Nathaniel "Nat" Dove is the last of the above group who was a student of Dr. Webster. He, too, started as a little boy, trying to play the family piano, and is now considered the quintessential bluesman in the business today. His list of contributions, credits, recordings and educational accomplishments is beyond the pages allocated in this chapter. However, some highlights are critical and are indicated here. Nat's credits include arranging, composing, producing and performing with many of the great blues personalities in America. He has traveled and played at various venues throughout the world. He founded the Bakersfield Blues Preservation Society to promote blues music as an art form through education. Some activities of the society include *Blues Alive*, a radio show promoting blues music in schools nationwide, and the Blues In the Schools Program. While living and working in Paris, he composed the musical score for the critically acclaimed play *Sail to Everest.* Nat studied music business at Columbia College, music broadcast communication at L.A. City College, film music at UCLA and music composition at New York University. One of Nat's recordings, "The Most Requested Rhythm Band," sold 750,000 copies. For a comprehensive view of Nat's range of work, see his websites: www.natdove.com and www.boogiebluesconnection.com.

Nat's success, as well as that of his fellow musicians, demonstrates how far African American students from E.A. Kemp Junior-Senior and Senior High have come since Bryan's early days of segregation.

Before ending this chapter, I have to mention Mrs. Johnnie P. Wyatt, E.A. Kemp's legendary music teacher and choir director, who was famous for the

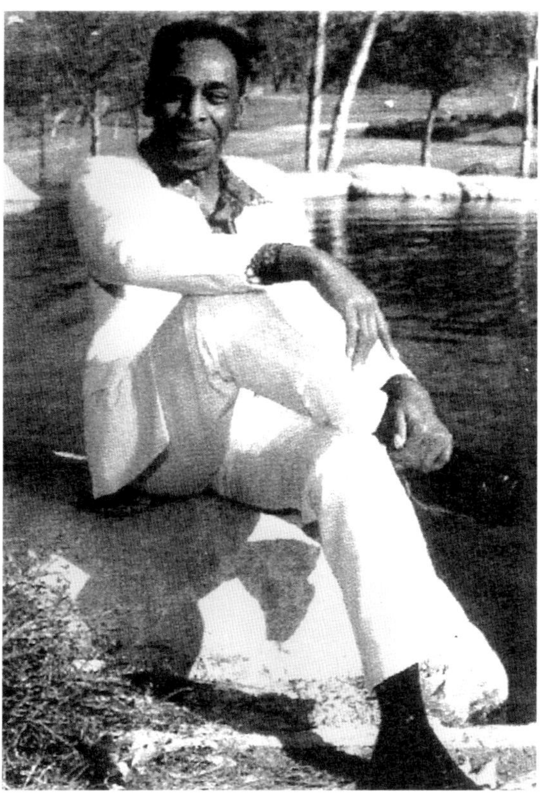

Walter Sterling Williams, a singer-songwriter and recording artist, sang in the E.A. Kemp High School choir. Today, he is a well-known blues artist and has released two albums: *Brand New Man, Grade A Quality* and *My Baby's Love. Courtesy Sterling Williams.*

school's prize-winning a cappella choir. One of her students, Frank Perry Jr., studied at the renowned Juilliard School of Music. Another student of hers, Sterling Williams (Walter L. Sterling as he was known at Kemp), is now a successful blues recording artist. Sterling has lived in both Chicago and Detroit and has played throughout the United States. He currently resides in Los Angeles. He is on the list of Soul Blues Artists and appears on Twenty-First Century Blues. His top albums are *Brand New Man, Grade A Quality* and *My Baby*'s *Love*. To learn more about Sterling Williams, see www.soulbluesmusic.com.

Author's note: Address information in this chapter is based on the 1990 E.A. Kemp High Class Reunion Directory, Bryan ISD Directory 2002 and personal interviews.

CHAPTER TWO

E.A. KEMP HIGH ALUMNI

Academic and Professional Achievements

However Tall the Mountain, There's a Road.
—Afghanistan

Dearest
We love and cherish, memories of
you—only you.
Hearts forever loyal to you, so royal
Our alma mater.
So will you, dear Kemp High,
Always inspire, guide and lead your
sons and daughters,
Give us consolation and inspiration
We love you, Kemp High—
Kemp High School
—E.A. Kemp High School Alumni Academic and Professional Achievement
Alma Mater

Given the humble living conditions, separate and "unequal" educational opportunities, many sons and daughters of E.A. Kemp Junior-Senior and Senior High Schools earned bachelor's, master's, doctoral and professional degrees in education, dentistry, law, medicine, pharmacy, social work and theology. In spite of limited resources, segregation and not being able to reach their potential, students demonstrated again and again that they could excel, as you will learn in this chapter and the ones to follow. Rather than being crippled or defeated by the social conditions of an unjust society, students were emboldened. The names of valedictorians and students who earned degrees and the institutions they attended reads like a who's who. Their names, specific degrees and year (where known) are noted.

Name	**Degree**
Darlene Sheppard Abrams	EdD
Ben Adams	BA
James Herman Alberson	BA
Willie Alberson	BS
Esterline Allen	BS
Henry Allen	BS (1960)
James M. Allen	BA
Lucille Allen	BA
Myrtle Allen	MA
Nora Allen	Bachelor's degree in Nursing (1960)
Sylvia Allen-Pouncy	BS Buisiness Mgt/Ed.
Willie Allen	BA
Linda Smith Asbury	MA and HS
Lennie Bailey	BA
O.D. Baker	Master of Education and Master of Theology
Luther Baldwin*	MBA
William Baldwin	Bachelor's degree in Business Adminstration
Cheryl Banks	BA
Janice Banks-Lightfoot	PhD
Blanche Barrow	BA
George Bell	BA, MBA
Barbara Bisor	BA

Nancy Bisor	BA
Robert Bisor	BA
Mary Frances Bradley	MA
Betsy Brown	PhD
Ruby J. Butler	BA
Andrew Byrd Jr.	MA
Samuel Callier	MDiv
Coakey Ellsworth Caroll	BA
Jesse Cashaw	PhD
Ikie Cashaw-Cooper	MA
Doris Green Coleman	BA
Pearl Collins	Master's degree
Edward L. Colquitt	BA
Rose Cowan	BA
Billy Cunningham	BS (1960)
Iney Cunningham	MA
Linda Cunningham	BA
Tommie Mae Dabney	MA
Andrew Truman Daniel	BA
W.C. Daniel	BA
Booker T. Davenport	BA
Willie Davenport	BA
Gwendolyn Davis	Master's degree
James Davis	BA
Nero Davis	BA
Wendell C. Davis Jr.	Doctor of Education
Fannie Herdon Diggs	MA
Chanie Dix	BA
Curtis Dix	BA

Doris Mae Dix	MA
Louise Dix	MA
Richard Dix	BA
Ruby Dix	MA
Barbara Williams Dixon	MS
Thelma Traylor Dove	MSN
Arthur Dunn	BA
Etta J. Duren	MA and HS
Vivian Murphy Duren	Bachelor's degree in Nursing
Davis Edwards	BA
Rosa L. Rouse Edwards	BA
Merion Ellis	BS
John Evans	Doctorate
Marilyn Evans	BA
Clyde Ferguson	MSW
Curtis Foley Jr.	BSN
Ethel Ford-Shipmon	MA
Wauline Pierce Gamble	EdD
Sid Garner	PhD
Waylon Garner	BA
Cleo Gilmore	BA
Drusilla Gilmore	BA
Ethel Gilmore	BA
Hiawatha Dix Godine	MA
Agnes Goins	BA
Inez Johnson Grays	MA
Zack Grays	MA
Alvin Green	MA Theology, Hon Doc of Theology
Frank Green	BA
John Green	BS

Lynda Green	BS
Milton Green	BA
Tommy L. Green	BA
Wanda Peterson Green	MA
Rosie Mae Rice Greer	MA
Ella Mae Groce	MA
Jerry Guyden	PhD
Robert Guyden	Master's degree
William G. Hall	MA
Carolyn Beatrice Hammond	MD
Charles Hammond	Doctor of Dentistry
Lovie Jewell Hammond	Doctor of Jurisprudence
William A. Hammond Jr.	MD
Winston Harnsberry	BA
Waldo Harnesberry	BA
Bettye J.D. Hatchett	MA
Merion Haynes	BA
Betty Jean Holland	BA
Daisy Ray Hollins*	
Walter Peter Hollins	MS
Ernest Hunter, Sr.	BSEE, MSEE
Bobbie Jean Idlebird	BA
Cari E. Idlebird	MA
Ivy R. Idlebird	BA
Joe C. Idlebird	MA
Maxine Idlebird	BA
James Irvin	MA
Wanda Jackson	MA
Woodrow Jackson	MA
Fred L. Jefferson	BA

Ruby Johnson-Abel	Master's degree in Elementary Education
Oletha Johnson-Bell	BA
Adolph Johnson Jr.	PhD
Bessie C. Johnson	MA
Bridgette Johnson ∫	Master's degree
Ellen Johnson	BA
Ernest Johnson	BA
Imogene Petty Johnson	MA
Juanita Gibbs Johnson	BA
Lillian Johnson	Bachelor's degree in Nursing
Melvin Johnson	HS
Wallace Johnson	BS
William Bruce Johnson	BA
Ernestine Johnson-Taylor	MA
Edna Jones*	BSN
Marilyn Jones	BA
Jo Ann Stephney Jordan	MA
Johnny Wesley Jordan	BS (1965)
Georgia Ann Kennard	Bachelor's degree in Nursing
Ann E. King	MS
Barbara King	BA
Lawrence King	MA
Alberta Biggers Knox	BS
Andrew Knox	MA and HS
Edward H. Knox Sr.	BS
Frederick D. Knox	BS, registered pharmacist and HS
Gloria Knox	BS
James Knox	BS and registered pharmacist
John Jerome Knox*	MA

Shirley I. Knox	Bachelor's degree in Nursing
Irene Randle Lane*	MA
John T. Lane	MA
John Latson	BA
Darcus Lightfoot*	Master's degree
James Lightfoot	Doctor of Divinity
David Littleton	BA
Vivian Faye Littleton	MA
Billy Joe Lockett	AA
Clarence Mack	BA
Dearest Mack	BA
Mazy Nell Smith Mack*	MA
Paul Madison	MBA
Catherine Martin	PhD
Freddie Mae Martin	MA
James E. Martin	BA
Helen McDowell	BA
Claddie McNeal	BA
Martha Miller	BA
George Mitchell	BA
Irene Shields Mitchell	BA
Jesse Monroe	BA
Mildred Monroe	BA
Esterline Moore	BA
Raymond Moore	MA
Thelma Moore	BA
Frankie Morris	BA
James C. Mosley	BS
Johnnie Mae Moten	MA

Lonnie Mulkey	MA
James T. Murphy	BA
Tommie Mae Murphy	MA
Ruth Neal	MA
Benjamin Nicks	BA
Milton Nowlin	BA
Royce Pace	BS
Roy Paul	BA
Bobby Joe Perry	MA
Effie Allen Perry	BA
Frank Perry	DA
Oswell Person	PhD
Robert Person	MA
Alandrus Peterson Jr.	MS
Hayward Peterson	BA
Pearlie Prunella Petty	MA
Blossie T. Phillips	MA
Calvin Phillips §	PhD
Eddie Mae Phillips	MA
Mildred L. Ross Phillips	BA, MA
Iona Potts	MA
Martha Potts-Scott	MA
Beatrice Potts-Young*	MA
Clovis Pruitt	MA
Vivian Vaults Rawls	BA
Mildred Ray	Master's degree and NHS
Jesse Rhone	BA + additional study
Henry Robertson	JD
Johnny Robertson	BA

Katha Robertson	MA
Jo Ann Robinson	BA
Kenneth Robinson	BA
Faye Patterson Sabbs	MA
Arthur Bo Sandle	BA Christian Studies
Jessie Sandle	AA, BA
Johnny Sandle	MDiv
Garfield Scott	BA (1960)
Claudette Scurry	Master's degree
Doris Stearne Scurry	MA
Lorenzo Scurry	BA
Beverley Sheppard	MM and HR
Carolyn Sheppard	MM and HR
Maggie Sheppard	
Robert J. Shields	MA
Sharon Shipmon-Kirwood	BS
Cheryl Shivers	BA
Hilda Shivers	BA
Albert Sims	Doctor of Jurisprudence
Ona Johnson Sims	MA
Altha Smith	Master's degree (1967)
Billy Ray Smith	MA
Eddie Smith Jr.	BA
Fred G. Smith	BA
Gladys Nell Green Smith	MSN
Willie C. Smith	BA
Lolethia Stearne	BA
James Sterling	BS, MS
Leroy Sterling	MA

Lorraine Sterling-Phillips	BA, MA
Shirley Steverson-Eaton	BA, MEd
Betty Suseberry	MA
Ernestine Suseberry-Hanks	Master's degree in Elementary Education
Edna Harris Tarrow	MA
Curtis Taylor	BA
Dorelia Powell Taylor	BA
Doris Ford Taylor	MA
Maxie Taylor	BA
Pansy Taylor	BA
Cora Hall Tennant	MA
Anderson Tennell	BA
Freddie C. Thomas	MD
Gwendolyn Thomas	PhD
Lloyd Thomas	BA
Doris Thompson-Foreman	BS
Janice J. Thurman	BA
Elmira Toines	BSN
Joe Willard Toliver	PhD
Melvin Turner+	BA
Opal Jewel Turner	BA
Sharon M. Turner	BA
Ethel Twitty	BA
Jesse Marvin Walker	BS
Bethenia Ellis Wallace*	MA
Charles Wallace	PhD
Gladys Sanders Wallace	MA
Ulysses Wallace	BA
Irma Jean Walton	BA

Jessie Mae Hunter Walton	Master's in Education
Karen Walton	BA
Odis T. Walton Sr.	Bachelor's degree
Odis Walton Jr.	JD
Weldon Walton	PhD
William Walton	BA
Halcyon Sadberry Watkins	DVM
Hiwatha Webber	BA
Cecil Webster ∫	MA
Madelyn Westbrook-Burley	MA
Amos L. White	BS
John D. White*	(1954) HS
Era Whitfield	BS
John L. Williams	MA
Marva Wilson	BA and NHS
Johnnie L.P. Wyatt	BA
George Vaults	MM
Queen Esther Vaults	BA

* Valedictorian
§ Transferred to Stephen F. Austin Senior Year
∫ Graduated from Bryan Senior High School
** Late Entry
HS Honor Student
HR Honor Roll
NHS National Honor Society
MM Denotes two master's degrees

Other E.A. Kemp alumni continued their education by attending such institutions as the American Banking Institute, Aspen Institute, Madam Coleman Beauty College, technical-trade schools and numerous other four-year and two-year colleges. They earned associate degrees, certificates, professional certifications and licenses required to practice in their respective professions, such as finance, management and nursing to name a few. Their accomplishments, in the same way as those listed above, demonstrate that they could move forward from behind, achieve and make meaningful contributions when given access and opportunity. The names of many of the individuals and the institutions they attended are listed below:

Hardie Allen
Velma Polk Allen
Ethel G. Batten*
Margaret Gibbs Brooks
Arthur K. Brown
Rastine Calhoun
Andrea S. Carroll
Donald Childs*
Nettie R. Clay
James Cooper
Leon Davis*
Lorenzo Davis
Nathaniel Dove
Tommie D. Duren*
Tommie J. Duren*
Johnny Ellis
Ruby Green Ellis
Freddie M. Ervine*
Willie D. Finley
Howard Gibbs
James O. Gibbs
Leroy Gibbs
Sarah Greer Graham*
James A. Green
Albert Griffin*
James Harnsberry
Sam Jackson
Jesse J. Jefferson
Jessie R. Jefferson
Donald Ray Johnson*
Autry E. Jones
Carolynne King
Grace King*
Edward H. Knox Jr.
Erie Lovell Knox
James Littleton
Lovie J. Littleton
Ollie R. Martin
Mary G. McClain
Ernest Moore
Jeffrey Nutall Moore
Jon Allen Mosley*
Charles Nelson*
Robert Newman
Brenda Patterson*
Waymon T. Peterson*
Isaiah Phillip
Earline Phillips
James Ray
Tarryline Richardson
Barbara J. Rucker*
Margaret R. Rucker
Conchita Sadberry
Collie Sander
James Sheppard Jr.
Sidney E. Simpson
Jackie Sims
Minerva Potts Smith*
Robert Smith
Laurence Stephney
Charles Sterling
Mary Frances Taylor*
Paul Toliver
Searcy Toliver
Geraldine Vaults
Mineola Vaults
Velma Vaults
John D. White
Erthel Wooley
Barbara Wright

* Late entries

Institutions Alumni Attended

E.A. Kemp alumni attended and earned their degrees from colleges and universities in the Midwest, North, South and West from the following institutions:

American Institute of Banking
American University (DC)
Antioch College (OH)
The Aspen Institute
Bishop College
Boston University
Bryan Vocational School of Nursing
California State University at Dominguez Hills
California State University at Hayward
California State University at Sacramento
City College of San Francisco
Clark-Atlanta University
Columbia University
Cornell University
Crozer Theological Seminary
Draughn's Business College
Fisk University
Gammon Theological Seminary
General Motors Institute (Michigan)
Hampton University
Houston Business College
Houston Community College
Howard University
Humboldt State University (CA)
Hunter College (NY)
Huston-Tillotson (TX)
Jarvis Christian College
Juilliard School of Music
Laney College (CA)
Lewis and Clark University (OR)
Lincoln University (PA)
Los Angeles City College
Metropolitan State College (CO)
Michigan State University
Milwaukee County Institutions
Mortuary Science College
Mountain View Community College
Northern Baptist Theological Seminar
Paul Quinn College
Pepperdine University (CA)
Prairie View A&M University
Prince George's Community College
Princeton University
Saint Mary's College of Nursing (AZ)
Saint Mary's University (San Antonio, TX)
Saint Philips College (TX)
San Francisco State University
Southern University (LA)
Texas A&M University
Texas A&M University Annex
Texas College
Texas Southern University
Texas Women's University
United States Naval Academy
University of California at Berkeley
University of California at Los Angeles
University of California at Santa Barbara
University of Chicago
University of Houston
University of Maryland
University of Northern Colorado
University of the Pacific

University of Southern California
University of Texas
Virginia Polytechnic State University
West Point Military Academy
Wilberforce University
Wiley College
Woodbury University
Yale University

Other African Americans not included previously, continued their education by attending Blinn College, Calvary Bible Institute and Seminary, Christian Life School of Theology, Grand Canyon University, Houston Community College, Laverne University, New Dimension University, Normandale Community College, Minnesota, Northwestern State University, Sarasota Academy of Christian Counseling, South Dakota State University, Southwest Theological Seminary, Fort Worth, Texas Southern A&M University, University of Houston, Webster University, trade and technical schools (e.g. Gulf Coast School of Real Estate and Tyler Barber College). They have earned certificates and degrees ranging from associate to doctorate. Names of the individuals are listed below in alphabetical order:

James Willie Ford Jr.
Alvin Green
Ernest R. Hunter Sr.
James Irvin
Bessie C. Johnson
Ernest Johnson
Wallace Johnson
William Bruce Johnson
Oletha Johnson-Bell
Rose Green Jones
Billy Joe Lockett
Prentiss Madison
Sylvia A. Pouncy
Arthur Sandle
Jesse Sandle
Johnny Sandle

CHAPTER THREE

EMPLOYMENT OPPORTUNITIES

Public and Private

PRIVATE JOBS

Education was not the only area of Bryan society that the separate and unequal doctrine for African Americans existed; the workforce was too. According to the city's website, "Bryan is a promising, thriving, forward looking city." This was not the case for African American residents in earlier decades. Employment opportunities were limited to only a few job fields, and most of these were at the bottom of the job well. They worked the dead-end, custodial, menial and pitifully low-paying jobs. Those who were employed as drivers for private van companies, telephone operators, chefs and head cooks and Lilly Ice Cream workers may have had better experiences, but these exceptions only made up a small percentage of the African American working class. The U.S. Post Office, although not in the private sector, was one if not the only business that did not require African Americans to use the back door for service. LaRue Johnson, Ples Turner, Odis Walton Sr. and Savannah Smith Williams (all World War II veterans) were a few of the first African Americans to be hired as mail carriers. But for a long time, African Americans could only find employment in janitorial-type roles, cleaning office buildings and polishing brass.

The reactivation of Bryan Air Base in 1951 did afford some jobs to area blacks but did not drastically change the employment situation. It's probably safe to assume that the few black men employed at the base earned a decent

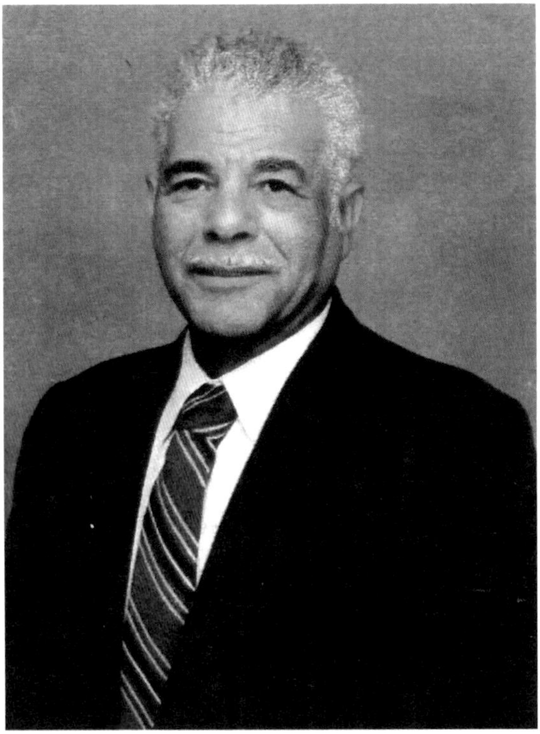

Ples Turner was a World War II veteran, a graduate of E.A. Kemp High School (1939) and was one of the first African Americans to work in the United States Post Office in Bryan, Texas. He was elected to the Bryan City Council and served for ten years. Turner was a home builder and quite possibly the wealthiest African American in Bryan at the time of his death. *Courtesy Daniel and Son Funeral Home.*

wage. Ocie Hall Sr. was one of the few individuals employed at the base. Robert Green and Otis Johnson were top cooks at the Charles and LaSalle Hotels in Bryan and presumably made good salaries. However, William Allen and Searcy Wilburn, bellhops at the hotels, earned very little. James Sheppard Sr. and Willie White were also top cooks, and it is assumed they received fair compensation. Arthur Adams was employed at the First National Bank, and Jack Green and Willis E. Ray were both employed at Roman's Pharmacy. Peter Davis and Fred Smith were employed at Vick's Pharmacy, and Leola Whitehead and Charlie "Womby" were both employed at the Palace Theater. Walter Hollins Sr. worked as the Bryan Hospital's elevator operator and also had other jobs.

Following are some of the numerous private businesses and companies in Bryan (and a few in College Station) that employed blacks:

A&M Waldrop
Borden Milk Company
Cade Motor Company
Caldwell Jewelers

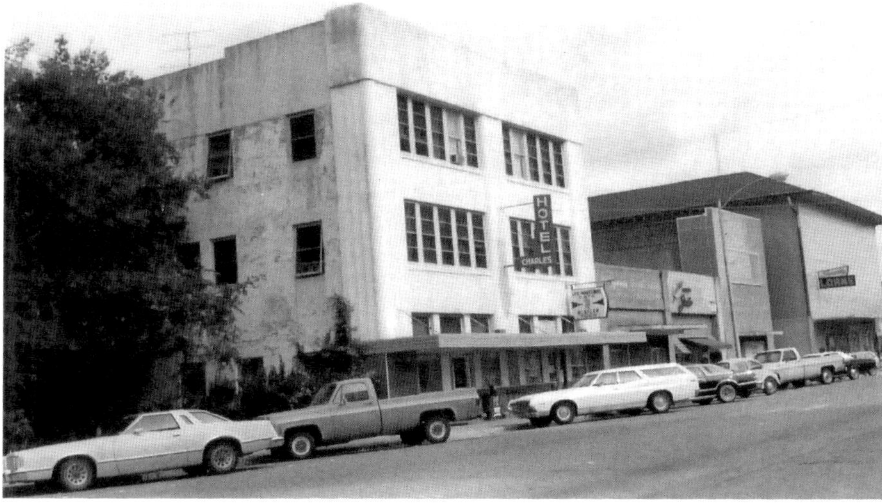

The Charles Hotel in 1980. The hotel was one of three located on South Main Street in downtown Bryan, Texas. *Courtesy Carnegie Center of Brazos Valley History.*

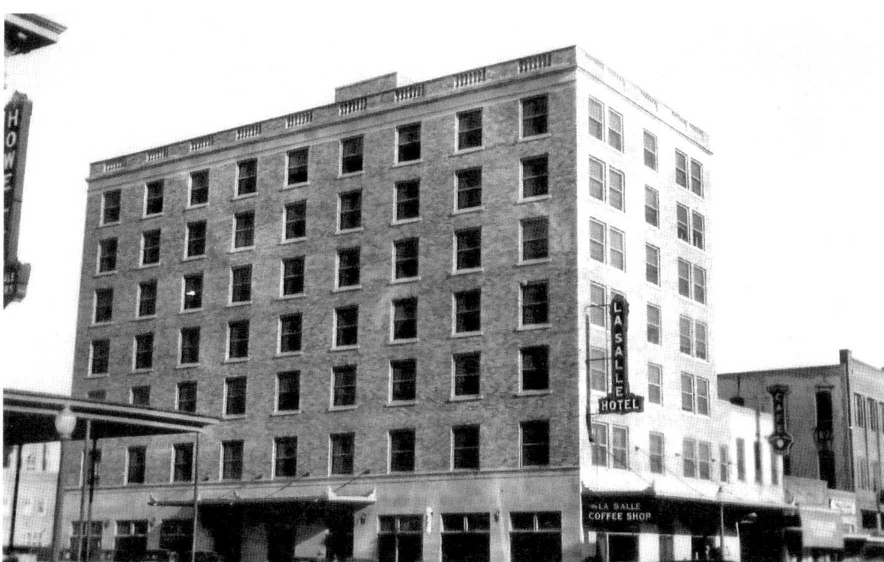

The LaSalle Hotel was built in the early twentieth century. In 1928, five more stories were added to the two-story building, making it the tallest building in Bryan, Texas. In its early years, the hotel did not permit African American guests. The hotel was added to the National Register of Historic Places on May 26, 2000. *Courtesy Carnegie Center of Brazos Valley History.*

Clothiers and Woodson Lumber Company
Coca-Cola
Corbusier Chevrolet
Dishman Pontiac
Dr. Pepper Bottling Company
Fabricare Laundry and Cleaners
Fashion Cleaners
Food Town Market
Haswell Motor Company
Holick's Boot Company
Howell Lumber Company
Humpty Dumpty Market
Kelley's Café-Restaurant
Kimbell Feed Company
Kraft Furniture Store
Major's Café-Restaurant
McCullough Dansby Furniture
Meat Locker Plant
Palace Amphitheater
Parker-Astin
Parker Lumber Company
R.B. Butler, Inc.
Roman's Pharmacy
Sanderson Farms
Sanitary Farm Dairies
Seven-Up Bottling Company
Sugar 'N Spice Drive Inn
Texas A&M University
Triangle Drive Inn
Varisco Lumber Company
Vick's Pharmacy

Private homes were another source of employment, primarily for African American women. Simply put, employment was limited and another challenging barrier blacks in Bryan had to overcome.

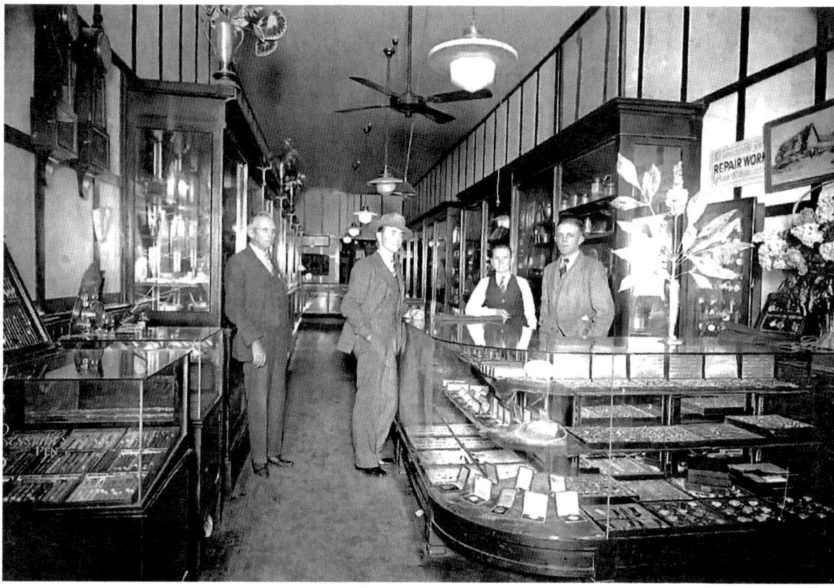

Caldwell Jewelers, located in downtown Bryan on South Main Street, was considered upscale and the most reputable jewelry shop in the city. James Johnson Jr., a World War II veteran, was one of the African Americans employed by the store. *Courtesy Carnegie Center of Brazos Valley History.*

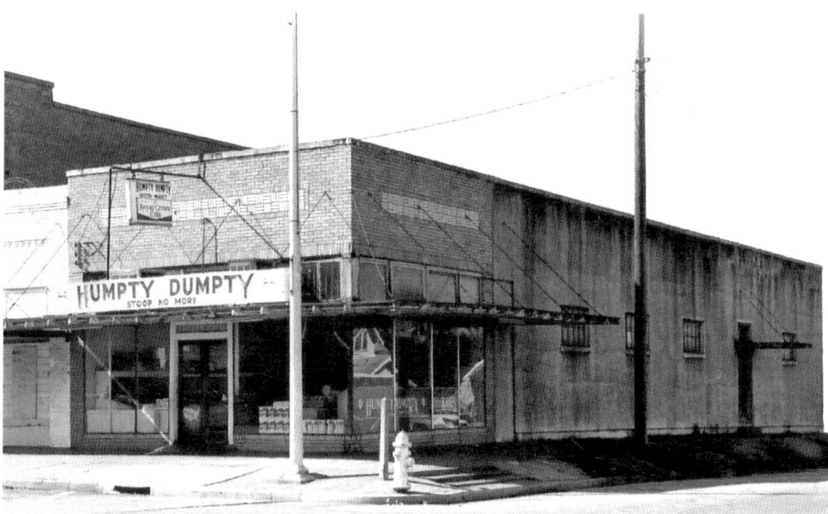

Photograph of Humpty Dumpty Market in downtown Bryan, located one block west of Main Street on North Bryan Street. The original store was built in 1915 and is still standing, but it is no longer operated as a grocery store. It was one of the downtown grocery stores that employed African Americans. *Courtesy Carnegie Center of Brazos Valley History.*

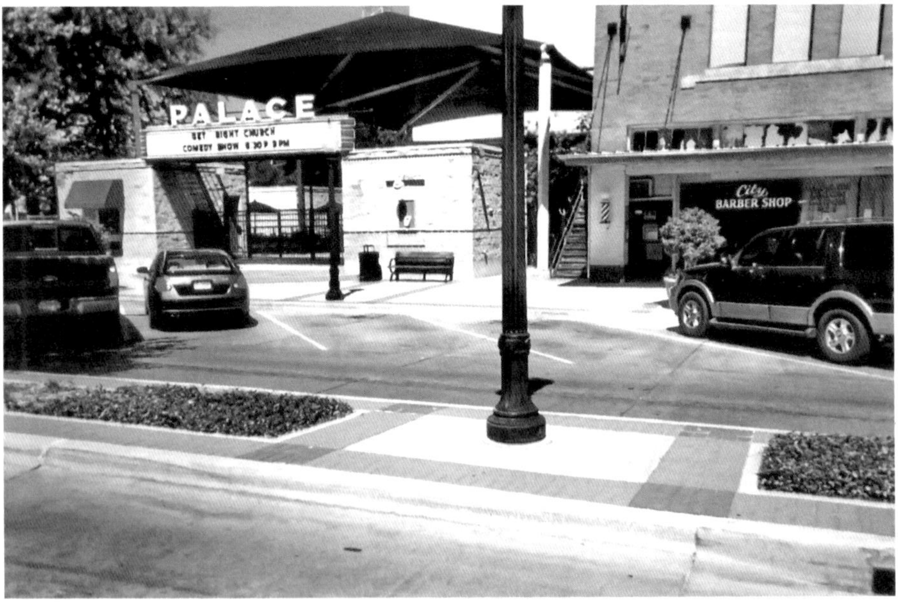

Recent photograph of the Palace Amphitheater on the original site of the 1928 indoor Palace Theater. It was converted into an amphitheater after the original Palace Theater burned. The amphitheater is currently the venue for city events. *Courtesy Carnegie Center of Brazos Valley History.*

PUBLIC

At first, the City of Bryan hired African Americans for menial jobs. Roger Harris and Jim Day, for example, were hired to clean dry toilets throughout the city. Maurice Green Sr., Eddie Phillips, George Banks and Joseph Dove worked on the sanitation trucks. Nathan McGee, Ollie Nelms, Roland Koontz and James "Sunny" Nash drove trash trucks; Terrence Bazy drove the brush truck. Maurice Green started his career with the city as a trash collector but retired as a supervisor after forty-five years of service. Other men who worked for the city in different departments include Ennis Owens and David Parker, who both worked in the Water Department, along with Olin Jenkins and Horace Patterson. Horace Nelson Sr., James D. Ray Sr. and Dave Woods all worked in the Public Works Department.

Willie Idlebird and Johnny Brown may have been the first African American police officers hired by the City of Bryan since Levi Neal. Levi

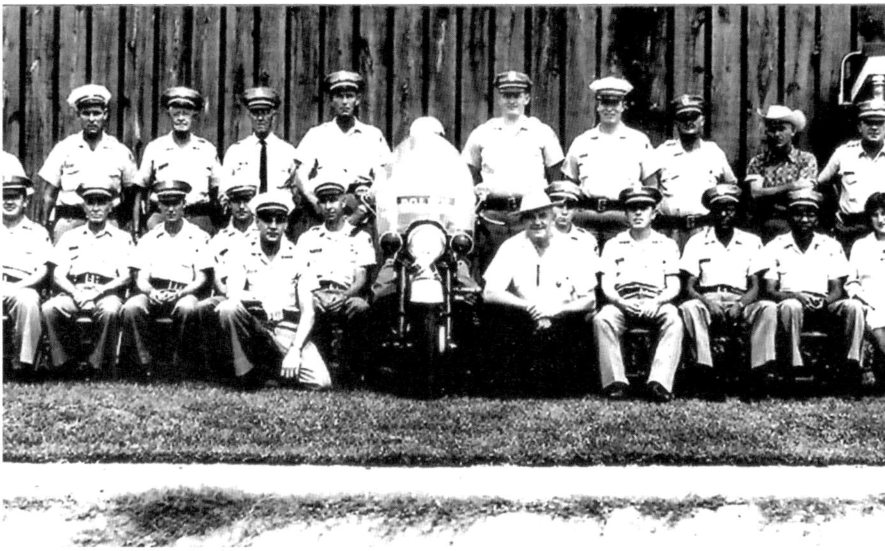

The Bryan City Police Department was established in the late 1860s. Pictured here are Willie Idlebird (third from right) and Johnny Brown (second from right), who were hired during the 1950s. *Courtesy Carnegie Center of Brazos Valley History.*

is reported to have served from 1880 to 1900 and had law enforcement authority over all citizens. However, at the time that they were hired, in the 1950s, they could only arrest "their kind." Two of the several other officers who followed Idlebird and Brown were Pinkey Hall and James T. Murphy.

Private businesses and city employment were not sufficient to sustain both the white and African American workforce, and many African Americans found themselves chopping and picking cotton in the Brazos River Bottom.

Private

Cotton crops were plentiful in the Brazos River Bottom where African Americans picked and pulled cotton. In some cases, entire families—fathers, mothers and children—worked in the river's bottom. Mothers, mine included, carried their babies to the cotton field, as they could not afford to pay someone to keep their little ones. The babies were placed on the cotton sacks and dragged as mothers picked and were taken off at the weighing scale. It was alleged that a Mr. Jackson and his family made enough money picking cotton to retire. Surely this was an exaggeration, but Mr. Jackson did boast openly of their weekly earnings.

Picking cotton was one of the most humiliating and back-breaking jobs performed by African Americans. They had to wake up very early in order to catch a truck that hauled them to the cotton fields. The cotton truck haulers were primarily African Americans and Mexican Americans. The more popular haulers were William Benford, Tom Butler, Charlie Perry, Will Sanders and his son Collie. Rudy Gregoria was the more popular of the Mexican American haulers. D.D. Catalena and Don Fazzino's brother were the two Italian Americans who hauled cotton pickers to their farms. The workday was from sunup to sundown in the brutal Texas heat. Picking cotton was made even more miserable by crop-dusters spraying DDT, which burned cotton pickers and stuck to their skin.

Working in cotton fields was not preferable, but for many families, it was the major source of income. Many, though not all, children were dependent upon the money that their parents made from picking cotton to purchase school clothing and supplies. In general, kids and parents from every sector of Bryan picked cotton. Willie Albert, Bass Butler, Lucas Luke, Mollie Hermon, "Sunny" Sanders, the Nelsons, the Wilsons, the McCoys, the Sterlings, the Childs, the Martins, the Perrys, the Henrys, the Davenports, the Turners, the Allens, the Wiliams and the Smiths were just a few individuals and families who picked cotton.

It was during the cotton days that Anna McCoy, my neighbor, introduced me to watermelon rind preserves and wiener spaghetti. She reared four grandchildren, three boys and one girl, after their mother died. Anna picked a little cotton and made meager meals to feed her grandchildren. One of the clever ways she fed the children was wiener spaghetti. She would buy a box of spaghetti and tomato sauce or paste and make enough to feed four children, plus a neighbor or two. She would sometimes buy a watermelon, and after eating the meat of the melon, she would use the rind to make preserves that the children often ate as breakfast.

After cotton farmers, one of, if not the largest private single employer in Bryan was the Allen Academy, formerly located on East Twenty-first Street. The Academy provided employment for the following men and their families: Wes Adams (also known as Wes Addison), Dolly Bisor, Andrew Brown, Valzay Brown, Willie Burton, Henry Dunn, Leroy Gator (who retired after fifty years), Rufus Graves, "Uncle" Mouton, Charlie Parnell, Tom Henry Rice Jr., "Doc" Rogers, Leonard Rouse, "Sunny" Sanders,

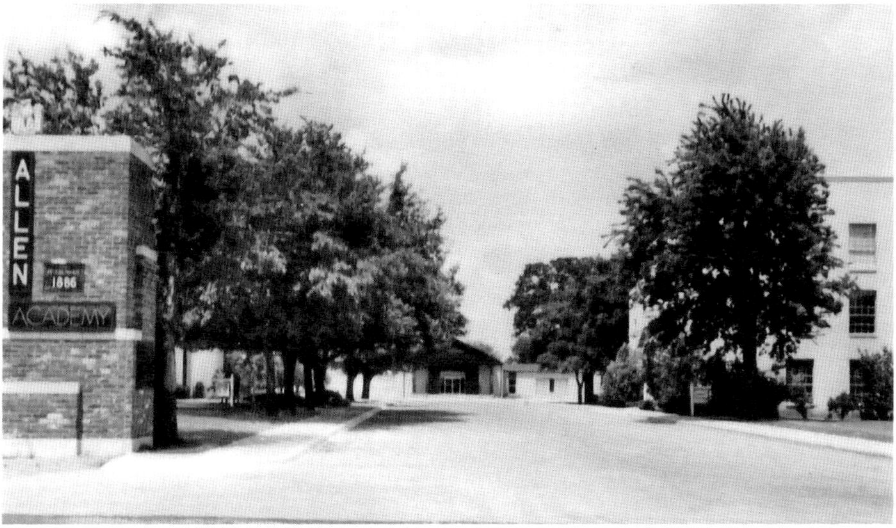

Allen Academy was originally called Madison Academy and was located in Madisonville, Texas. It became Allen Academy in 1896 and moved to Bryan in 1899. For many years, it was a major employer of African Americans. *Courtesy Carnegie Center of Brazos Valley History.*

W.D. "Screwball," Archie Sims, Freddie Watson, Freddie William, Earl Williams and Ira Williams. I also worked at the academy for a time. Texas A&M University (then called Texas A&M College) was another source of employment for some African Americans. For example, Charlie Mason was a "top cook" in the university's dining hall, the Memorial Student Center (MSC) Bowling Alley and the cafeteria. Julia Shields also worked in the university's dining hall, and Son Coleman, Vivian Peterson and Parthenia Smith worked in the university's laundry facility. William Smith and I set bowling pins in the MSC. Herman Brown and Robert Shields worked in the MSC before they enlisted in the U.S. Navy, and Leroy Gibbs worked in the MSC before he enlisted in the U.S. Air Force. Other African Americans from Bryan also worked at Texas A&M, but their names are unknown. The university also employed large numbers of African Americans who lived in the city of College Station.

CHAPTER FOUR

AFRICAN AMERICAN VETERANS

World War II, Korea and Vietnam

According to the *Bryan Daily Eagle*, over six hundred African American men and women left Brazos County to serve in World War II between January 19, 1941, and August 20, 1945. The majority of them were from Bryan and served in the army, but a few served in the navy. According to T.C. Battle, African Americans have served in the military as far back as 1639. But this chapter will focus primarily on those who served in World War II, Korea and Vietnam.

Many African American sons and daughters left Bryan to serve in a war, traveling to places some of them had never even heard of, only to return to the same segregated place they had left. They fought, bled and died on the continents of Africa, Asia and Europe, only to come back home to unchanged educational, employment and housing conditions. However, their experiences exposed them to travels and different points of view. For example, some GIs, such as Luther Bell, Clayburn Greer, James Johnson and Isaiah Martin, moved to the West Coast and Pacific Northwest and never returned to Bryan. They found job opportunities in the shipyards, and some worked at Boeing Aircraft. Some found a better life in San Francisco, Portland and Seattle, while others moved to Detroit, Illinois and Philadelphia looking for jobs, homes and better lives for their children.

Some (not all) of the names and a few photographs of the men and women from Brazos County—black and white—who served in World War

II are listed in a book entitled *The Men and Women in World War II from Brazos County and Aggie Veterans*. Listed below are the names of only the African American veterans, most of whom were from Bryan or attended E.A. Kemp Junior-Senior High School.

Billy Anderson
Joe A. Bernal
Raymond Bowser
Willie M. Bowser
Johnny Brown
Charlie Buchanan
Isaac Buchanan
James L. Buchanan
Benny Calhoun
Thomas Calhoun
Henry Carter
Roosevelt Clopton (O)
Benny Cunningham (PH)
Frank Ellis
Jonathan Gay
Isaiah Gooden
Lesley Green Jr.
Rodney Green
Steve Green
Toy Green (PH)
Andrew Griffin
Arthur D. Hamilton
Edgar Hamilton
Arthur D. Hawkins
Lavaughn Hawkins
Albert Hayes
B.L. Johnson (K)
James Johnson
Nathaniel Johnson
Obie Jones
James Kennard
Otis Laws
William A. Laws
Fred Martin
Ocil McGee
Andrew Mitchell
W.Z. Nelson (PH)
Sandford Nutall (PH)
Billy Parker
Henry Parker
Ernest Payton
Tommie L. Person
Lamar Porter
"Bubba" Rayford
John H. Robertson
William T. Ross
Richard Shaw
Willie Shaw Jr.
Daniel Smith Jr.
James Smith
Jester W. Smith
L.C. Smith
Woodrow W. Smith
Willie Stephen
Archie Suseberry Sr.
Robert L. Thomas
Tollie N. Thompson
Curley Thornton
Daniel O. Toliver
Searcy Toliver
Herbert Wallace
Emmett Walton
Rayfield L. Whitman
Burnise Williams
Richard Williams Jr.
Woodrow Wilson
Randolph Wright Jr.

An incomplete list of other World War II veterans, not mentioned above, including women who served during World War II, is included below.

Elijah Adam
Luther Bell
H.B. Buggs
Richard Childs
John Robert Clay
Odessa Clopton
Lonny Deere
Samuel Ellis
Wilson Anna Elmore
Milton Gree
Clayburn Greer
Milton Gross
Della Harris's brother (K)
Virgil T. Hickman
J.D. Hill
Clancy Jones
Needie Jones's son
C.W. Kennard
Lawrence King
Benney Leon
George Lewis
Eugene Littleton (PH)
Isaiah Martin
Jessie M. Newsome
Url Ocheltree
Alandrus Peterson Sr.
Virgil Peterson
Leon Pillows
Johnny Robertson
Columbus Robinson
Paul Scott
Clarence Sterling
James Thomas
Ples Turner
Lawrence Wallace
Marvin Walton
Odis T. Walton Sr.
Samuel B. White
"Sonny Man" White
Herman Williams
Savannah Smith Williams
Joyce Wooley

O Officer
K Killed
PH Purple Heart

A special note was published on page two in the December 5, 1942 edition of the *New York Amsterdam*:

> *A Master Sergeant at the age of 23 in less than three months is a record established by Edgar L. Sadberry of Bryan, Texas. Edgar earned a Bachelor of Science in Agriculture from Prairie View College and was the brother of Oliver Wayne Sadberry, Principal of Washington Elementary School. The Sadberry brothers a total of seven, were all college graduates.*

After the war, the government sponsored three vocational training sites for professional barbers, mechanics and tailors. African American veterans interested in becoming barbers attended the site located on the corner of Twenty-second and North Bryan Streets. Jettie Parks was the manager of the training site for barbers. Veterans interested in learning how to become tailors trained at the site located on West Nineteenth and North Bryan Streets. The manager for this site was John L. (Lev) Thomas. Veterans interested in mechanics trained at the site located on West Nineteenth and San Jacinto Highway. H.K. Hornsberry was the supervisor for this site, and Ernest Moore was one of the certified instructors. When the mechanics training was discontinued, the building was converted to the Three Aces Night Club.

Many of Bryan's African American citizens also served in the Korean Conflict. Some of the young men were drafted their senior year of high school, while others volunteered. A few of the ones who were drafted returned after the conflict and received their diplomas. Some of the names, not all, of the sons and daughters of E.A. Kemp High who served during the Korean Conflict include:

Betsy Brown
Claude A. Brown
Ernest Brown
Franklin Brown
Herman O. Brown
Fred Burton
Ralph Campbell
Freddie Carter
Ollie Carter
Vernon Chambers
Odessa Clopton
Sloan Clopton
Edward Colquitt
James Cooper
L.C. Davis
Wendell Davis
Adam I. Donaly
Joe Dupree
Curtis Duren
H.P. "Frock" Emanuel
Eugene Garvin
Leroy Gibbs
L.C. Gipson (killed)
Stanley Griffin
Benny Gross
James Harnsberry (WO)
James Harrison
Virgil T. Hickman
Lester Lee Holland
William Hughes
Woodrow Johnson
Benny Jones
J.W. Jones
Fred Douglas Lewis
Roosevelt Littlejohn
Robert "Billy" Martin
Curtis Miles
Ira Mitchell
M.L. Mitchell
Ernest Moore
Mavis Morgan
Sam Mosely Jr.
Eugene Nixon
Lawrence "Big Boy" Nutall

Neal Nutall Jr.
Felix Petty
Waldo Quarles
Homer Rice
Tom Henry Rice Jr.
Nettie Mae Richardson
James Eddie Rooks
Robert J. Shields
Andrew "Buddy" Smith
Joe Solomon
John Steen
Ray Steen
Archie Sueberry Jr.
Samuel Taplin
Hampton Taylor
Willard Taylor
Paul Toliver
Samuel Walker
R.C. "Bucket" Wallace
Arthur Walton
Paul Walton
James Aaron Ward
Hiwatha Webber
Freddie Williams
Herman Williams Sr.
Levi Williams
Marion "Buck" Williams
Dan Wilson
L.C. Wyatt
Robert Wyatt

Some of the same veterans who served in Korea also served in Vietnam; their names are listed below, along with the men who served in Vietnam:

Charles Allen
Willie Allen
Frank Asberry
Otis Asberry
Raymond Asberry
Jeff Bailey*
Michael Bailey
Arthur "Bo" Benford
Leslie Benford
Charles Blackshear
Claude A. Brown*
Herman O. Brown*
Milton Carroll
Charley Carter
Otis Carter
Lorenzo Cashaw
James Cooper*
Herman Crenshaw
Booker T. Davenport
Robert Dunn
James Willie Ford Jr.
Leon B. Gafford
Harold Gainous
Sid Garner
Howard Gibbs
Larry Grays
Lemuel Grear
Alvin Green
Ennis Green Jr.
Howard Green (PH)
Maurice Green Jr.
Virgus Green
Albert Griffin
Ocie Hall Jr.
Harvey Hanks
James Harnsberry (WO)*
Arthur Heads
Lonnie Heads
Fred Herdon
Norris Ray Hill
Lou James Hines
Leon Houston (PH)
Shedrack Houston
William Hughes
Ernest R. Hunter Sr.
Peter Lee Hunter

James Irvin
Cleo Jackson
Edward Jackson
Bessie C. Johnson
Donald Ray Johnson
Ernest Johnson
Joe Nathan Johnson
Lancy Johnson
Raymond Johnson
Wallace Johnson
William Bruce Johnson
Marion Jones
Rastine "Foxall" Jones*
Frederick Knox
Clinton Lewis
Billy J. Lockett
John Lougeridge
James E. Martin
Robert "Billy" Martin*
Robert McGhee
Curtis Miles*
Willie S. Mitchell
Willie Morrow (WO)*
Benjamin Nicks
James E. Nixon
Ernest Parker
John Parker
Shelton Parker
Curtis Benford Perry
James Benford Perry
James Rayford Perry
Waymon T. Peterson
Bobby Phillips
Charles Phillips
Isaiah Phillips
Robert Phillips
Homer Rice*
Jerry Rice
Arthur Ross
McArthur Ross
Jesse Sanders
Arthur Sandle Sr.
Jesse Sandle
Johnny Sandle
Robert J. Shields*
Clarence Simpson
James Simpson
Albert Sims
Charles Smith
Willie C. Smith
Edward Stephney
Johnny Stephney
Perry James Stephney
Maxie Taylor
Clarence Thomas
Elijah Thompson
Melvin Thompson
Robert Thornton
Nolan Turner
Roger Turner
Elvin Walker
R.C. "Bucket" Wallace*
Tollie Waller
Alvin Walton Jr.
James Emmett Walton
Cleotis Ware
Richard Warren
James Watson
Clarence Williams
George Riley Williams
Henry D. Williams
Willie E. Wilson

WO Warrant Officer
*In service during Korean Conflict

CHAPTER FIVE

SMALL BUSINESS OWNERS

African Americans and Italian Americans

Many African Americans owned a variety of small businesses that provided them a level of independence, although they could not escape the limitations of segregation. Nonetheless, they were far better off than African Americans who were fully dependent on white business owners for employment. Between the years 1880 and 1910, black barbers, butchers and grocers provided services to the black community. According to Olivia Banks, black commerce, which included merchants and craftsmen, only made up about 10 percent of the heads of black families. Apparently the rest of the population held menial jobs, such as farmers, day laborers and domestics.

African American Businesses in Downtown Bryan and on the East Side

Bryan was a geographically divided city, with African Americans occupying the north end of the city and also part of both the east and west sides. In downtown Bryan, their small businesses were concentrated between Twenty-first, Twenty-second and North Bryan Streets. However, as you will see later, there was a variety of businesses in and throughout the neighborhoods.

Most of the downtown businesses consisted of professional barbershops, taxicabs and a variety of other businesses. For example, the following barbers were downtown: Hilbert Clopton, Henry Crawford, W.R. McQueen, Tommy Murphy, Jettie Parks, Jeremiah Smith, Searcy Toliver, Burney Goosby and Charlie Moseley. Downtown taxicab operators were Henry Jenkins, Fred Martin, Milas Moore, O.C. Parks and Alton Thomas. Henry Jenkins, Bailey Brown, Sarah Reid, Garfield Scott and Walter King operated cafés, and Ed Pigford and John L. "Lev" Thomas had real estate offices. John L. also operated a dry cleaner's and tailor shop. Dr. Samuel J. Sealey Sr. had a medical clinic on the second floor of a building that was owned by Henry Jenkins (also known as Poppa Jenkins). Clyde Gilmore owned a records shop next door to Henry Jenkins, and Will R. McQueen owned a pool hall. J.S. Foster drugstore was located at 1906 North Main Street, and Dr. S.W. Hooks, a physician, owned a drugstore on Caldwell and Bryan Streets in a building that was owned by Italian businessman Parks Noto. White and Thompson owned a drugstore located at 2311 Main Street. Dr. William A. Hammond Sr. operated a medical clinic and office on the corner of Twenty-first and North Bryan Streets.

There were three beer taverns downtown, two of which were between Twentieth and Twenty-first Streets (operators unknown) and a third one on North Bryan Street that was operated by Henry Haley. Ray Tarver owned a café on North Bryan Street.

There were a number of small business owners on the east and west sides. Starting on the east side, Mary Adams owned a laundry on Dansby Street that provided employment for Willie Freeman, Erie Lokelton, Vivian Peterson (my mother) and Parthenia Webber Smith. Rossetta Johnson owned a barbecue pit, café and beauty shop. The boy who lived with her, James "Sunny" Johnson, helped in the café. If you made friends with him, he would share some of the café's spoils. Julia Shields owned Bob's Confectionery, where delicious malts and hamburgers were made, and it stocked a few grocery items, too. In addition, it had a jukebox, and that made the confectionery a very popular spot for young people on the east and west sides. Her son Robert and her daughter Minnie operated the business. Odis T. Walton Sr. owned the small Candy Hill Grocery Store before serving in World War II. Not very long after he returned, he built a commodious store on the corner of Candy Hill and Pierce Streets. The store no longer exists, but when it did, it was well stocked with a variety of meats, dairy products, dried and canned goods, notions, produce, hunting items, tobacco products and kerosene and gasoline. He also owned several apartments next to the store.

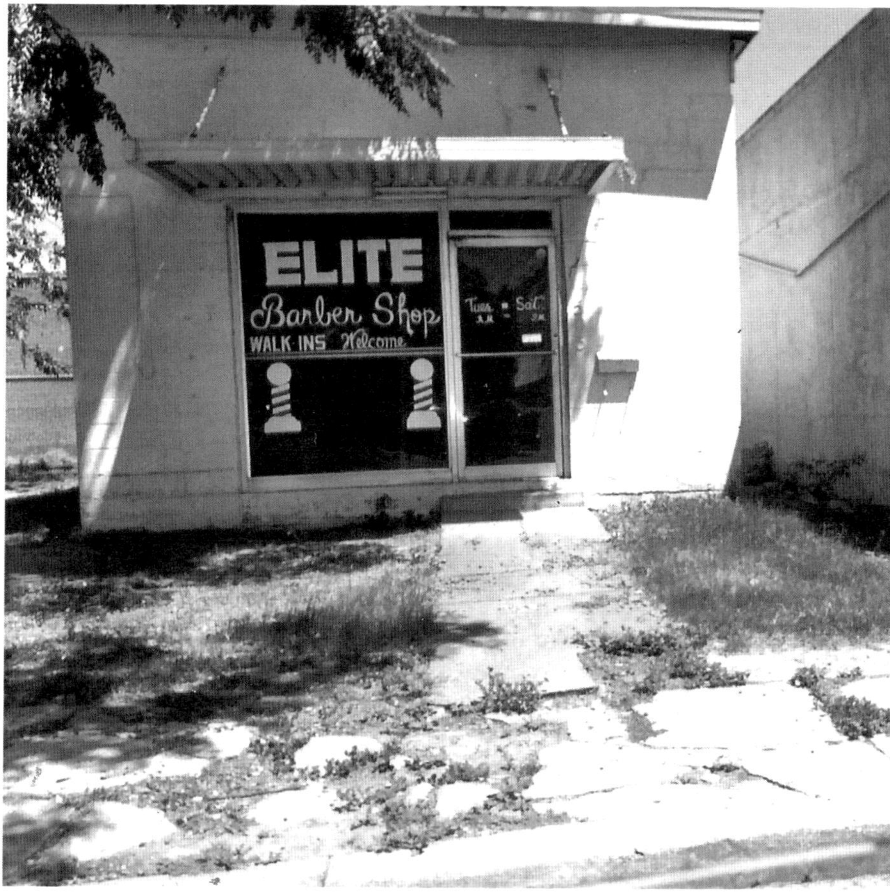

Elite Barber Shop was one of many barbershops on the north end side of downtown Bryan, where most African American businesses were concentrated. It was owned by Henry Crawford in 1925 and was operated by Jettie Parks and Marcellus Stewart in 1946. It was operated by Searcy Toliver in later years. *Courtesy Brazos Valley African American Museum and* Up from Cotton.

Odis Walton was more than a grocery store owner: he was an entrepreneur. He owned another grocery-type store on South Pierce Street, about four blocks from his Candy Hill store. The store was sold later to Joe Restivo's son and converted into a beer tavern and café. The tavern was operated by "Sonny Man," and his parents ran the café. The tavern was frequented by adults who listened to Howlin Wolf, Muddy Waters and other "Gut Bucket" music. The café was where the young crowd congregated and treated themselves to plates of smoked sausage and sweet potatoes, one of the specials. The tavern was later managed by Eddie B. Booker. Ernest H. Cass, mentioned above, was manager of the Universal Life Insurance Company.

On East Nineteenth Street (now MLK Street), Odis owned a confectionery and Jean's Sewing Shop and had an apartment on the second floor. He also owned the OK Motel. Jean's Sewing Shop became a shoe-repair shop operated by Roy King in later years. After the shoe shop, it became a beauty shop and was operated by Pearlie Mae Murphy. The confectionery/café eventually became a U.S. Post Office and polling place.

P.J. Stearne owned a grocery store on East Nineteenth Street that was previously owned by Lester Cunningham. His store was stocked modestly with a variety of meats, produce and dairy products and was where students from Washington Elementary School could buy lunch. P.J. later sold the store to Don Fazzino, who continued the practice of selling lunch to students. Guy and Bruce Barrow owned a grocery store on Henderson Street, and Pete and Sonny Man White's mother operated a small café-like store on East Twenty-first Street. It mostly sold sodas and potato chips, but it was a fairly popular place because young people could dance to tunes on the jukebox.

African Americans owned convenience stores on both the east and west sides before they were very popular. These stores were conveniently located in the immediate neighborhood and carried such items as bread, milk, snack foods, sodas and ice creams. There were four convenience stores on the east side: Tom Peterson and Clayburn Greer Sr., located on the corner of Weaver and Pierce Streets; Emmett Walton, located on the corner of Branch and Pierce Streets; and William Groce's store on Waco Street.

Johnny Robinson, a World War II veteran and the first African American master plumber in Bryan, owned a plumbing business on the east side and hired J.C. Davis to work for him. Jordan Nelson also owned a plumbing business on the west side and hired Will Smith to work for him. "Doc" Henderson and C.W. Kennard owned a concrete business and provided employment for John D. White, who was in college at the time, and two of Mr. Henderson's sons.

There were three funeral homes in Bryan owned by African American morticians. Ed Scott owned two locations of People's Undertaking Company. In 1937, one location of People's Undertaking Company was at 111 East Twenty-third Street. In 1939, the second Undertaking Company was located at 700 North Houston Street. In 1947, the name was changed to Scott Funeral Home, and the address was 501 East Twentieth Street. After Mr. Scott's death in the 1950s, a group of local African American men purchased the funeral home, Lawrence King and Ural Ocheltree among them. Mr. Carey Cauley became the funeral home owner after King and Ocheltree, and the address was changed to 609 North Houston, but Cauley retained the name.

Reverend Wesley C. Daniel Sr. owned Bryan Undertaking Company, which was located at 700 North Sterling Street on the west side. In 1951, the name was changed to Daniel Funeral Home, but it remained at the same address. Sometime between 1970 and 1971, after the death of W.C. Daniel Sr., the funeral home name was changed to Daniel and Son. In 1971, W.C. Daniel Jr. and Inez Robinson established a new Daniel and Son Funeral Home, which was located at 401 West Eighteenth Street. Today, it is owned by Kenneth Robinson and Betty Robinson. In 1952,

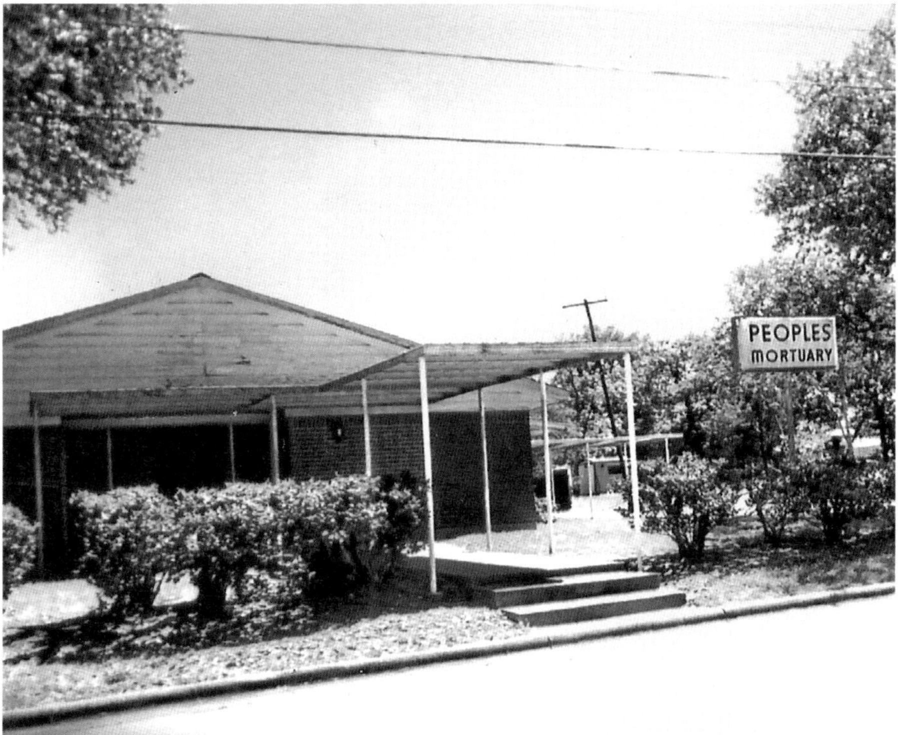

Formerly the People's Undertaking Company of East Twentieth Street, owned and operated by Ed Scott. After his death in the 1950s, it came under group ownership, and the name was changed to the People's Funeral Home. The last owner, Carey Cauley Jr., changed the name to People's Mortuary, and the address was changed to 609 North Houston Avenue. Today, the funeral home is in disrepair and is no longer in operation. *Courtesy Oswell Person.*

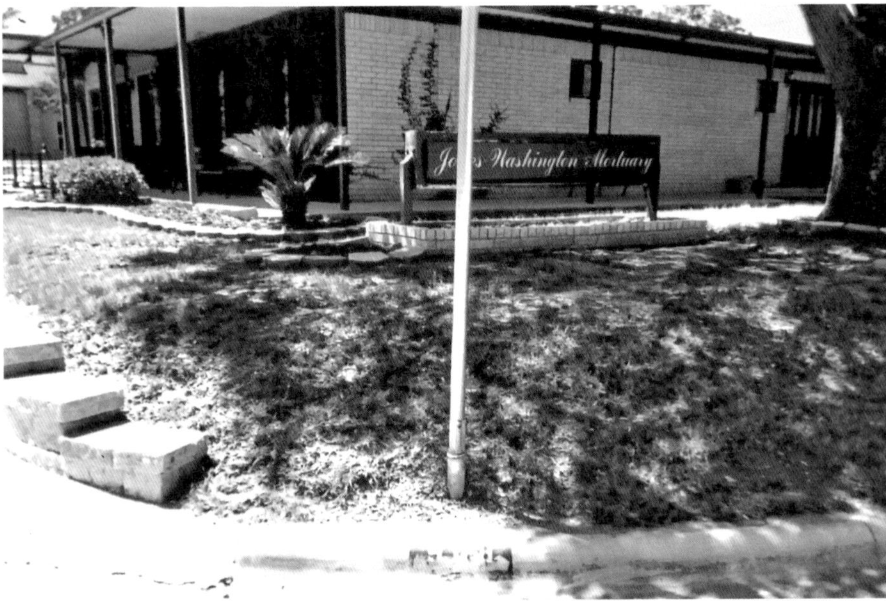

In 1952, Gus Jones built Jones Mortuary in Bryan on a lot located at 508 East Nineteenth Street. Jones sold the funeral-mortuary to a Mr. Washington in 1975, at which time, with permission from Mr. Jones, the home was renamed Jones-Washington Mortuary. The home remained in the same location for thirty-seven years. *Courtesy Jones-Washington Mortuary.*

Guss Jones built a third funeral home and named it Jones Mortuary. The funeral home was built on a lot purchased from Mr. Restivo and was located at 508 East Nineteenth Street. In 1975, after Mr. Jones died, a Mr. Washington bought the business and, having received permission prior to Mr. Jones's death, changed the name to Jones-Washington Mortuary. Other African American entrepreneurs were Jimmy Bell, who was assistant supervisor for the Atlanta Life Insurance Company; Ernest H. Cass, who worked for Universal Life Insurance Company; S.B. Redden, who sold life insurance; and W.C. Daniel Sr., who owned a funeral home and, as mentioned above, also sold burial insurance.

There were four day-care centers owned by African Americans on the east side: Lula Dean, Minnie Bennie, Helen Simpson's Candy Hill Day Care and Betty Suseberry Hank's Life Long Learning Center. Lula Dean's Day Care was located on the corner of East Twentieth and Houston Streets. Helen Simpson's Candy Hill Day Care was located on Pierce Street. Minnie Bennie's Day Care was located on East Nineteenth Street at the corner of

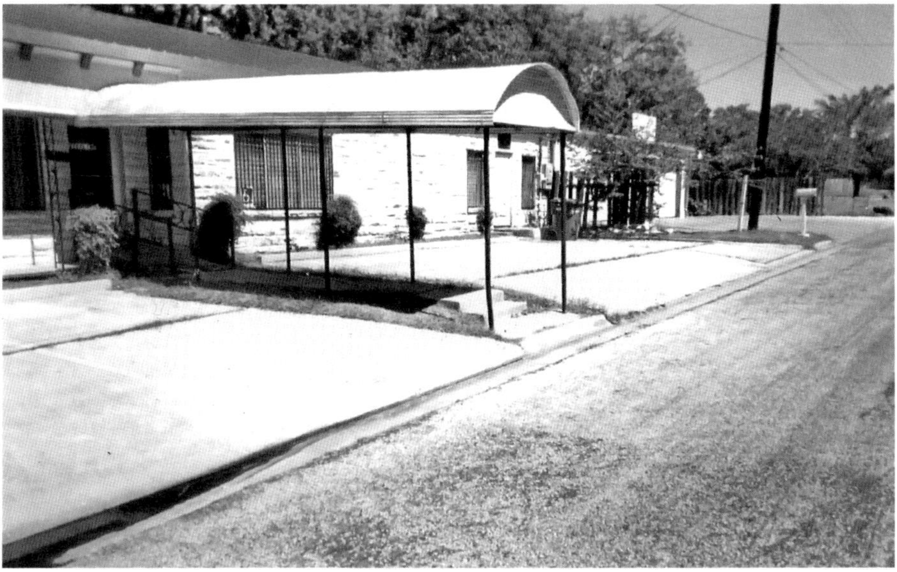

W.C. Daniel built a funeral home in the 1940s known as Daniel and Son Funeral Home. The building was originally a frame structure, and a brick façade was added in later years. Not too long after W.C. Daniel Sr. died, Mr. W.C. and Inez Daniel established another Daniel and Son Funeral Home, located at 401 West Eighteenth Street. It is currently owned by President Kenneth and Vice-President Robinson. *Courtesy Daniel and Son Funeral Home.*

Highway 6 South. Betty Suseberry Hank's Life Long Learning Center is still located on the corner of East Dansby and Bradley Streets.

Grocery and Convenience Stores on the West Side

Sam Mosely's Grocery and Market, located on West Nineteenth Street, was comparable to Odis Walton's Candy Hill store in every way with one exception: he provided home delivery. He also owned several facilities. One was rented by John R. Clay for his shoe-repair shop. Another was a café/restaurant (which was operated by Horace Nelson). The rest was other rental property. Elmer and Lindsay Grays owned a modest grocery store located on San Jacinto Highway between Seventeenth and Eighteenth Streets. Rachel Cavitt owned a grocery store on West Nineteenth Street near San Jacinto

Highway. Fred Evans was owner of a grocery store located on West Twenty-eighth Street. Clarence Johnson and Fred Martin operated a convenience store located on Florida Street, and Jody Neal owned a convenience store near Doll's Beauty Shop, which was on West Nineteenth Street and was similar to the ones located on the east side. Robert Jones operated a place located between West Seventeenth and Eighteenth Streets that was similar to Mrs. White's place on East Twenty-first Street. T.C. Calhoun owned Calhoun's Grocery on West Muckleroy Street.

BARBEQUE PIT OWNERS-OPERATORS ON THE EAST SIDE

Barbeque pits were popular business and often owned by African Americans. There were a minimum of eight located on Bryan's east side. Henry Elarms's place was on Pierce Street, Aaron Johnson's was on Twentieth Street and Rosetta Johnson's (no relation) was on Dansby Street. William "Rag" Mathis's Bar-B-Que Hut once sat on the corner of East Nineteenth and Preston Streets. Will Nettles's pit was on Eighteenth Street, the Four-Way Inn and Modern Club was on East Nineteenth Street and Lester Nowlin Bronx Café was on Eighteenth Street. May Atkins was another barbeque pit owner.

BEAUTY SHOPS AND BARBERSHOPS ON THE EAST SIDE

African American beauty shops were plentiful on the east side, starting with Nettie Richardson Clay's Beauty Shop on Preston and Twenty-first Streets. There was also Birdie Davis Green's shop (Birdie was a graduate of Joyce and Cecil Wooley's Beauty School) on Waco Street, and Rosetta Johnson's shop (mentioned earlier) was on Dansby Street. Lelia Latson, Cassie Rice and Joyce Wooley had a beauty shop on Pierce Street, and Aslee Sims and Annette Idlebird Stephney operated the Pierce Street Shop. Joyce also had a barbershop on Pierce Street. Pearlie Murphy's shop was on East Nineteenth Street. Gertie Randle and Cecil Wooley owned beauty shops on Henderson Street, and Cecil's husband, Mr. Wooley, had a barbershop on Henderson Street too.

Barber and Beauty Shops on the West Side

Eugene Garvin and Robert Newman owned barbershops on West Nineteenth Street. Garvin's shop was near George Washington Carver Elementary, and Newman's was near Scanlin's Market. Alice Ellis had a barbershop on West Eighteenth Street, and Carrie Walker's shop was on Twenty-eighth Street. It is probably safe to assume that, given the number of beauty shops (salons), African American women cared about their beauty and hair. In addition to the shops located on the east side, Doll Sanders Mosley and Erie Knox both owned beauty shops on West Nineteenth Street (Edna Neal, Ella Green and Nancy Murphy were the operators for Mosley's shop). Lillie Dunn and Lorraine White owned shops on or near Harlem Lane, and Beulah Young owned a shop on Lucky Street near San Jacinto Park. Jessie Rae Jefferson Nelson owned a beauty shop and café on San Jacinto Highway near the corner of West Seventeenth Street. B-Neat Beauty Shop, owned by Bessie O. Matthews, was located on West Seventeenth and Columbus Streets, and Leona Blackshear had an in-house shop on West Twenty-first Street.

Cafés, Diners, Snack Bars and Restaurants on the West Side

Cavitt's Café (which was later converted to a beer tavern) was on the corner of West Twenty-first and Sims Streets. Scott's Diner was located on West Twentieth Street and was owned by Garfield and Jessie Scott. Littleton's Snack Bar was owned by Earl and Alma Littleton. The Blue Dine Inn was owned by Horace Nelson Sr. and was on West Nineteenth Street. Richard Childs and Jessie Rae Jefferson owned cafés on the corner of San Jacinto Highway and West Seventeenth Street. Lizzie Green owned

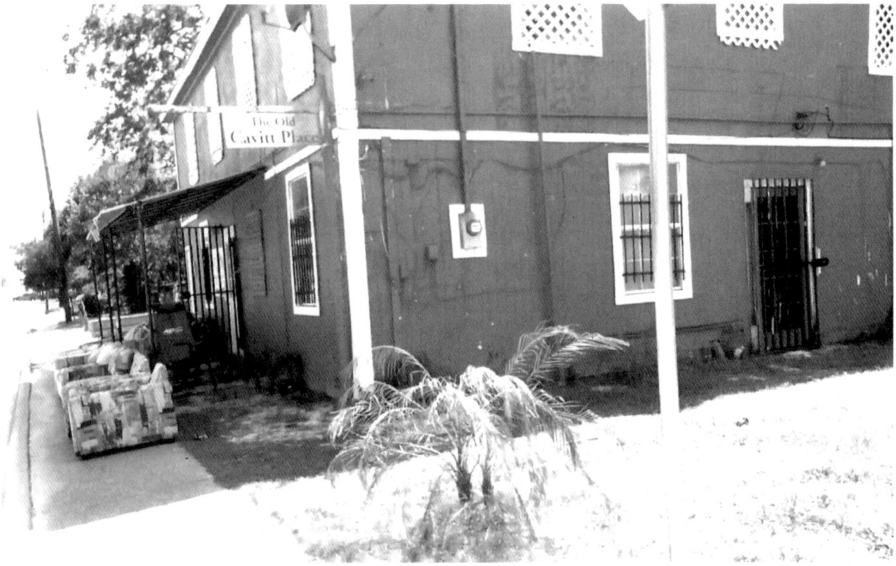

Pictured here is a building that is today known as the Old Cavitt Place. In the past, it was Cavitt's Café, a nightclub and a furniture store. In spite of its age, the structure is still sound, and through all its different designations, it has remained on the corner of West Twenty-first and Sims Streets. *Courtesy Oswell Person.*

a café on West Twenty-second Street, and Phillip's Café and Barbeque was located on Saunders Street. Scott's Diner was the eatery for out-of-town athletic teams that competed against E.A. Kemp High School. It was also a popular spot among Kemp's faculty and students. The Scotts also operated a café in downtown Bryan on the corner of Main and Twenty-first Streets.

Littleton's Snack Bar also provided lunch, but mostly to students. Mr. Littleton's son James and daughter Faye worked the lunch hour during school. She was generous. When some students (including me) could not pay the full price for a lunch, she accepted what they could pay. Later, while in the navy, I attempted to show my appreciation by sending magazines and other small gifts while she was attending college. Littleton's was more than fast food; it was a place where benches were provided so that young people could congregate after school and on weekends. The snack bar was also a place of employment for students like Adolph Johnson Jr., Robert Richardson Jr. and Dewayne Mosley, and I even worked there while waiting to attend college. Bessie Shannon owned a barbeque-café that was originally located on West Nineteenth Street near San Jacinto Highway. The place was relocated to Peale Street and is currently under the management of her daughter as a café only. Rosie's Barbeque was located on West Nineteenth Street, and Charlie McNeil's Barbeque was located on West Sixteenth and Hall Streets. In addition to his barbershop, Eugene Garvin owned a snack bar.

Garages, Scrap-Metal Junkyards, Service Stations and Other African American Businesses

Nick Benford owned a scrap-metal junkyard located on the corner of Dale and Candy Hill Streets, and Henry Clay also owned one on the corner of Henderson Street and Military Drive. Charlie Perry owned a scrap metal yard on Houston Street in Freedmen Town. Henry Carter operated a body shop and garage on the corner of San Jacinto Highway and West Seventeenth Street, and Steamer Johnson's garage was located about three blocks north of Carter's shop. Elmer and Lindsay Grays owned a large garage about two blocks south on San Jacinto Highway. Earnest Walker and James Taylor owned service stations, and Taylor's service station had a garage attached. Both were located on West Nineteenth and San Jacinto Highway. Earnest Walker also owned a Gulf Service Station on San Jacinto and Jenkins Street. Milton Turner may have owned the only African American body and paint shop in Bryan. Rastine Calhoun operated a scrap-metal junkyard on Saunders Street near San Jacinto Park, and Isaac Madison also operated a junkyard. Tom Thornton owned a garage on West Nineteenth Street near North Bryan Street.

In addition to the businesses mentioned above, African Americans owned dry cleaner's, hotels, laundries, radio/television and shoe-repair shops in downtown Bryan and on both sides of the city. Rastine Jones operated a dry cleaner's downtown on North Bryan Street. Chester Adams owned O.K. Cleaners and Laundry on the corner of East Eighteenth and Highway 6 South, not far from Williams' Hotel. The largest dry cleaner's and laundry operation was owned by Dr. William A. Hammond Sr. It was a modern plant that included pickup and delivery service and was located on West Seventeenth Street. James Hedge was the proprietor of the West End Cleaners on West Nineteenth Street. Vern Mayo and Rachel Cavitt also owned a dry-cleaning service on West Nineteenth Street. John Robert Clay had the distinction of owning and operating two shoe-repair shops, one between East Twenty-first and Preston Streets and the other on West Nineteenth Street. Roy King operated his shop on East Nineteenth Street, and Aaron Butts's shop was on the west side near Lucky Street. Roosevelt Lucky owned a television shop on Saunders Street, and Lewis Rice owned a radio repair shop on the west side. Dr. William A. Hammond Sr. operated a kindergarten facility near the hospital. Rosetta Cheeks owned a day-care center on Columbus and West Eighteenth Streets. Mr. and Mrs. J.W. Bell owned the Ding Dong Bell Kindergarten and Nursery on West Seventeenth Street. Felix Jones may have been the only African American in Bryan who owned a house relocating business. Dossie Foster was owner of another O.K. Cleaners that was located on North College Avenue.

Nightclubs, Beer Joints and Taverns

Other small businesses that were owned and operated by African Americans in Bryan were places to buy and drink beer and for the over-twenty crowd to socialize. Some nightclubs were referred to as "beer joints" because they did not qualify as nightclubs based on the opinions of the community. Such establishments were located on both sides of the city. One was the Cotton Club, located on the east side just off of Waco Street, which was owned by "Fatty" Robb. It was a very popular spot in the late 1940s and was revived intermittently during the late 1950s. The Four-Way Inn, located on East Eighteenth Street near Highway 6 South, was known as a honky-tonk. It had a reputation for catering to a rough clientele and was where a number of citizens met their demise, including Daniel Morgan. Of the three beer joints downtown, Henry Haley operated the one on North Bryan (mentioned earlier) that attracted a rowdy crowd. Owners-operators of the other two are unknown. The Night Spot, another beer joint, was located on East Tabor Street and was known for being a dangerous place. In fact, citizens known to me were mortally wounded in this establishment.

The Tin Shack, located at East Seventeenth Street and Highway 6, was another beer joint that attracted a rowdy crowd. The Hole in the Wall, operated by Hazel Coleman, was located on Pierce Street near East Nineteenth, and it attracted a variety of clients. On the corner of Washington Street and Highway 6 was another unsavory beer joint. Charlie Perry operated a beer joint in Freedmen Town near Highway

6 and East Eighteenth Street and the Big Apple Night Club on West Nineteenth Street and San Jacinto Highway. Richard Childs operated a popular nightclub on the corner of West Seventeenth Street and San Jacinto Highway that is now a seafood store. On Seventeenth Street and down from Richard's Place, "Buddy" Caldwell operated a night spot. A block from Buddy's was the Tick Tock Club, which was operated by Zellie Newton. Harmon "Son" Bell operated the Blue Moon Club located off San Jacinto-Highway 21 extended. The Merry-Maker was on West Highway 21, beyond the Blue Moon. Odis Walton Sr. was thought to be the owner. Ennis Green operated a beer joint and rooming house on Hall Street, and McGee's Hotel was on San Jacinto Highway. Lizzie Horn operated a rooming house on the west side on or near California Street. Beyond these Bryan establishments, some adults traveled to Frank Banks's Friendly Five Tavern in College Station. Others would go a few miles north to a popular spot called the Tea Room in Hearne, a city located in Robertson County.

Italian Americans: Small Business Owners

According to sources, early Italian immigrants came to Texas through New Orleans, Louisiana. Most of them were Sicilians. They settled in the Brazos River Valley and learned cotton farming; however, many of their children and grandchildren left cotton farms and moved to Bryan and became businessmen. Some of them could have been the children and grandchildren who lived and owned businesses in African American neighborhoods (mentioned earlier). The following Italian Americans lived or owned businesses in African American communities:

Don Fazzino owned a grocery store on East Nineteenth Street that he bought from P.J. Stearne. He also owned the Harlem Drive Inn, located between West Twentieth and Twenty-first Streets, as well as the Modern Club on East Nineteenth Street. Both of these establishments attracted a more sophisticated clientele. Jake Cangelosi, Niock Dalio, Tony Boatcallie and Mike Ruffino owned grocery stores on the east side. Niock Dalio also owned a beer joint on East Nineteenth that attracted an older and less urbane crowd. Tony owned a beer tavern on Pierce and Bradley Streets that attracted a demographic similar to Niock Dalio's place. Jake Cangelosi

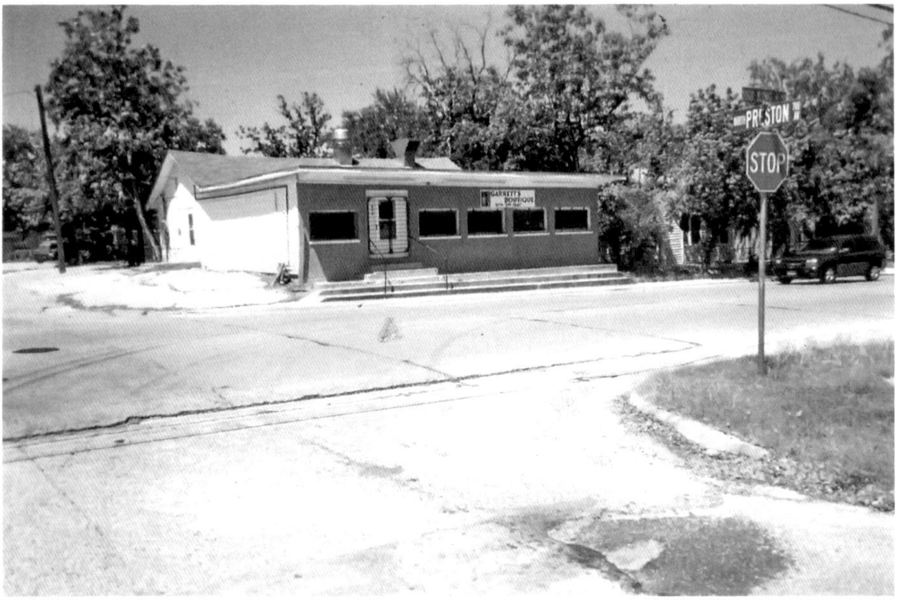

In the 1940s, Mr. P.J. Stearne sold the grocery store located on East Nineteenth Street that he had bought from Mr. Lester Cunningham to Mr. Don Fazzino. The store was near Washington Elementary School, and since the school did not have a cafeteria, Mr. Stearne sold lunchmeat, saltine crackers and sodas to students for fifteen cents. The new owner, Mr. Fazzino, continued the practice. Today, the store looks just as it did in the 1940s, except for the brick façade. *Courtesy Oswell Person.*

owned a grocery store near Washington and Apple Streets and Highway 6 North. Charles Fererri did not actually live in the neighborhood, but he owned the Sugar 'N Spice Drive Inn located on Highway 6, just north of Washington Street.

Another Italian American whose last name was Ferro owned a grocery-deli that was located at 309 West Twenty-first Street. Joe A. Restivo owned a grocery store at 400 East Nineteenth Street. The original store was demolished and replaced with a convenience gas station–type store by one of his sons (the same one who bought Odis Walton's Store on North Pierce Street and converted it to a beer joint and café). Luke Graffizi, Johnny Lampo, Charles Ruffino and Frank Scanlin (of the Market Store, formerly owned by the Collettes family and known as Collettes' Grocery) were all grocery store owners who lived in African American neighborhoods on the west side. In African American neighborhoods where Italian Americans lived and/or owned businesses, they provided employment for members

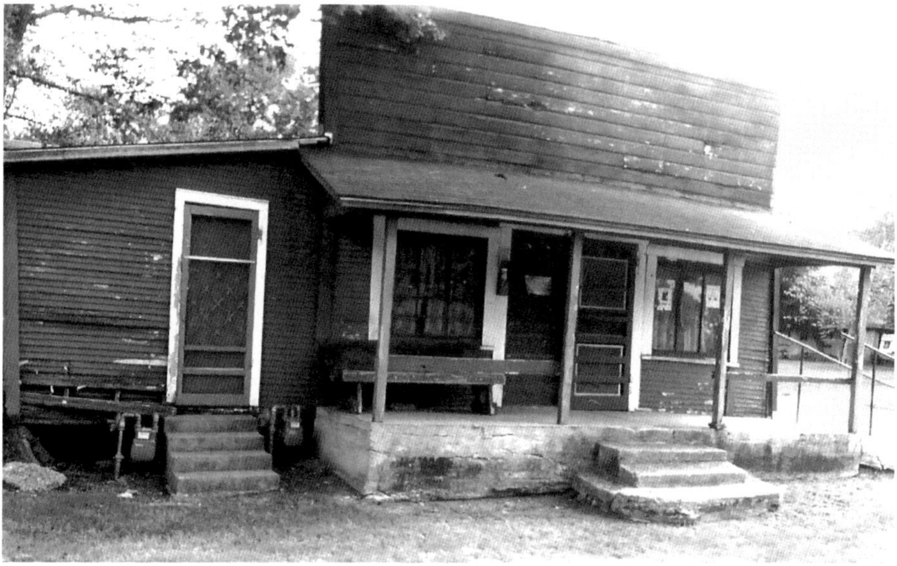

Early 1940s picture of Niock Dalio's grocery store, located on East Nineteenth Street. He was one of a number of Italian Americans who lived and owned businesses in African American neighborhoods. The store is still standing, although time has caused some deterioration, but it is no longer in operation. He later added the section on the left as a place for African American customers to purchase beer and play dominoes. *Courtesy Oswell Person.*

of the immediate community. For example, Jack Johnson, Arthur Dunn and Anne King worked in the grocery store or in some other capacity for Don Fazzino. Vernice Turner and Ruby Davenport worked at the Harlem Drive Inn, and Joyce Thompson worked at the Modern Club, which was also owned by Don Fazzino. James Banks, James McCoy, James E. Martin, Charles Sterling, Leroy Sterling and Bunny Wright were employed by Charles Fererri. Tony Boatcallie employed Mrs. Rosetta (last name not known), and Tommy Traylor, Frank Perry and Rudolph Johnson were employed by Frank Scanlin.

CHAPTER SIX

SHOTGUN RENTAL HOUSES AND GOVERNMENT PROJECTS

The limited employment opportunities for African Americans in Bryan prevented many from paying school taxes and purchasing homes. Many blacks, consequently, lived in rentals. Both African Americans and whites owned and rented substandard three-room houses that were referred to as "shotgun houses," so called because you could see through them. Most of theses houses, but not all, were unpainted and lacked running water, indoor plumbing, wallpaper and window treatments. Even though the houses were substandard, they kept families (mine included) from living on the streets or being homeless. My family was eventually able to purchase a lot and build a little house on the corner of Branch and Pierce Streets, eliminating our dependency on such housing. But we did live in two different shotgun houses, one on Henderson and another on Dansby Street, both on the east side of Bryan.

Starting on Dale Street, Elliott Myers Sr. owned two or three rental houses. One was occupied by Ida Davis and her children: Johnny, Mickey, Jean and Sunny. The second house was occupied by Lillie Mae Brisby, Cleveland, Frank, two sisters and sometimes their grandmother. When Ida Davis vacated the house, one of the Mitchell sisters and her family assumed occupancy. Three additional families, the Blues, Browns and Thurmans, occupied the house after the Brisby family. Farther south on Dale Street, near Middle Street, Joyce Wooley's brother and his family lived in one of three shotgun houses. Charlie Crawford, his wife and her daughter lived on the same block.

Dyke Hicks, his wife, Bobby, and his sister lived in the last house on Dale Street near Candy Hill Street. On the corner of Candy Hill and Dale Streets were several houses that were occupied by the Coleman, Thompson, Blue and Mitchell families. Lee Doris Jones and her daughter lived farther south on Dale, near the corner of Bradley Street.

On Bradley Street, directly behind Lee Doris, lived a man named Mr. Watson. The Walton family lived nearby, on Bradley and East Twenty-first Streets. Both 1940 vintage houses are still occupied. There were four more unpainted houses on Dale Street close to Military Drive that are no longer there. Two were occupied by individuals whose names have been forgotten. The third house was occupied by the Gator family and the fourth by a woman named Roxanne and her sister.

East of Dale, on Pierce Street, were three rental houses where bachelor Cornelius Kilpatrick and two friends, Gibson and Harris (first names unknown), lived. Gibson owned a mule and was hired out to plow gardens, and Harris had been married to Della Lewis. C.L. Smith lived directly behind these three men, on Candy Hill Street.

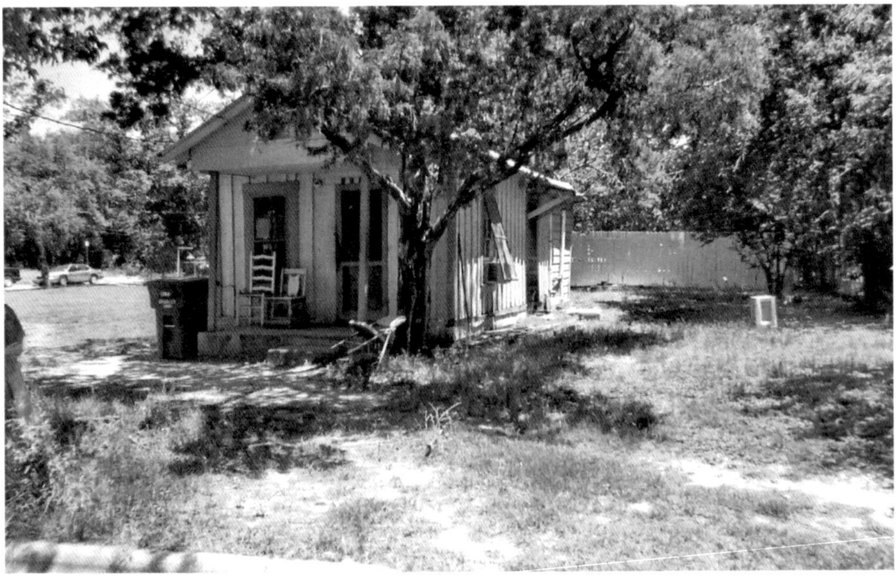

Picture of a typical shotgun house, so called because one could see straight through the house, from front to back. This house, located on East Bradley Street, was built during the late 1930s and early 1940s. In the early 1950s, it was home to a bachelor named Mr. Watson, and as of June 2012, a different individual occupies the house. *Courtesy Oswell Person.*

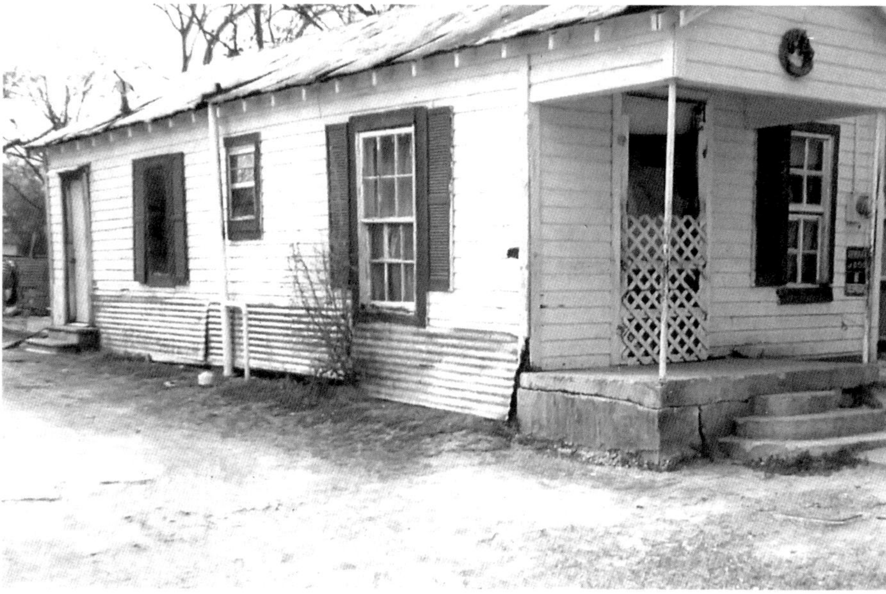

Mr. A. Walton and his family of four or five children were occupants of this shotgun house, built in the 1940s. The house is on East Bradley, near Twenty-first Street, and is still occupied by tenants today. Plumbing hardware, which has been added since its original construction, can be seen on the house's exterior. Since shotgun houses did not have inside toilet facilities, families had to build outhouses. *Courtesy Oswell Person.*

Continuing south on Pierce Street, past Bradley Street, were four or five more shotgun houses. The first house was occupied by a woman known as "Sweet Momma" and her two sons; Clarence Ross and Bertha, his wife, lived next door. Next to them lived Ira Williams, his wife and two sons. Emmadine and her family lived in the fourth house. There was a cluster of similar houses behind these four, one of which was occupied by a man called A.J. and his family. I believe James Otis Henry's relatives lived in the next house, and at one time, Freddie Williams, his wife, Dorothy, and their daughter also lived in the same cluster.

Approximately two blocks farther down on Pierce, at the corner of East Nineteenth Street, was a group of houses where relatives of Aubrey Hill lived. The Nixon family and Sunny Caldwell's sister and son also lived in one of these houses (separately, of course). Making a U-turn on Pierce where Henderson Street terminates is Waco Street. People who lived on this street were quite proud of their community, but some of them were subjected to the same poor housing conditions as many others in Bryan.

Arthur Brown, his mother and sister and her family occupied two separate shotgun rental houses that were on North Henderson Street near Pierce Street. On the opposite side of the street, Rose Loud and her two sons occupied a shotgun house that was owned by Rose Castle or Henry Elarms (reports differ). Willie Mae Adams and her daughters lived on the same block, and Roland Hunter and his mother lived three doors down from Willie Mae, next to Juanita Mundine Nix, whose house had a different architectural style. Two blocks from Roland were three houses, all of which were owned by Elliott Myers and an individual named Tom Ware. Two of the houses were occupied by two families by the name of Sterling and Phillips; my family occupied the third house. Mary Addison owned one unpainted shotgun house across the street that was occupied by two different Smith families. Eddie Smith Sr. and his family were one of the first occupants, and Gladys Smith and her family occupied it after Eddie Smith.

The corner house at the end of Henderson Street and Military Drive was occupied by a man whose nickname was "Chummy" and who died in a fire. A veteran of the Korean Conflict and his wife lived across the street from Chummy. In the same block heading westward were three more houses. A boy named "Skeeter" and his mother lived in one, and the Henrys lived next door. Who occupied the third house is not known. As of October 2009, the Henrys' house was still there and was occupied by its new owner. During a recent trip to the old neighborhoods, I noticed that three shotgun houses are still standing, grim reminders of unpleasant housing experiences from years past.

There were two shotgun rental houses on the first block of North Twenty-first Street (near the original New Zion Baptist Church). One was occupied by Doris and her brother Israel. The occupants of the second house were unknown. Pearl Forward owned several of the same type of house on Twenty-first Street, where the street intersects with Dansby Street, but hers were painted. As I recall, Christine, her daughter Jo Ann and her son Dan occupied the one next to the Fennells. My mother, sister and I lived across the street from Christine, and the Baileys and Dorseys lived next door. James Otis Henry and his father lived in the last house on the first block near the corner of Dansby and Candy Hill Streets. At the end of Dansby, on Military Drive, were three more houses. The first house was occupied by Johnny Floyd and his parents, the second house by his grandparents and the third house's occupants were not known.

West of Military Drive was Freedmen Town, a community with a large concentration of shotgun houses. Families who lived in Freedmen Town experienced similar if not the same poor housing conditions. Near Shiloh Baptist Church, on the side of Houston Street where Earnest and Corrine Cass lived, were three or four shotgun houses. Joe Turner occupied one house, the Perrys lived in a second house and another Turner family occupied the third house. Emmett Matthews lived on the corner of East Eighteenth and Houston Streets.

About a block up from Freedmen Town, on Houston Street, were more houses occupied by another family of Perrys, as well as the Browns: Lenora, Leroy, "Brother" Minnie, Howard and his wife. Pauline and her family lived off Highway 6 South and Seventeenth Street.

Many of the same kind of rental houses seen on the east side were also seen on the west side. The exceptions were the ones owned by Dr. William A. Hammond Sr., which were painted white with green trim, his signature colors. The houses on Boulevards Street near Highway 6 North and on San Jacinto Highway up toward Twenty-second Street were mostly occupied by low-income families. The same was true for cross streets, including Sims, Logan, Sterling, Randolph, Congress Hall, Hudson, Dean, Harlem Lane, Florida, Murkleroy and streets in between.

Government Projects

Construction of government projects began on a site adjacent to Carver Elementary School in the 1950s. This may have marked the first time many families had running water, paved streets and semi-central heating and air conditioning. For many, including my family, living in the projects was a huge step up. However, getting a rental unit was not so easy, as the demand for housing exceeded availability. In order to get one, it was often necessary for applicants to have someone with some influence in the community vouch for their character. Still, applicants who worked for the City of Bryan or well-to-do white families were often granted units first. The demand for decent housing eventually became so great that a second phase of government projects was built opposite the site near Carver Elementary School on West Nineteenth Street.

Construction of government housing began on the east side shortly after the second phase of construction was completed on West Nineteenth. These projects were constructed on East Twenty-first Street, at the end of Dansby

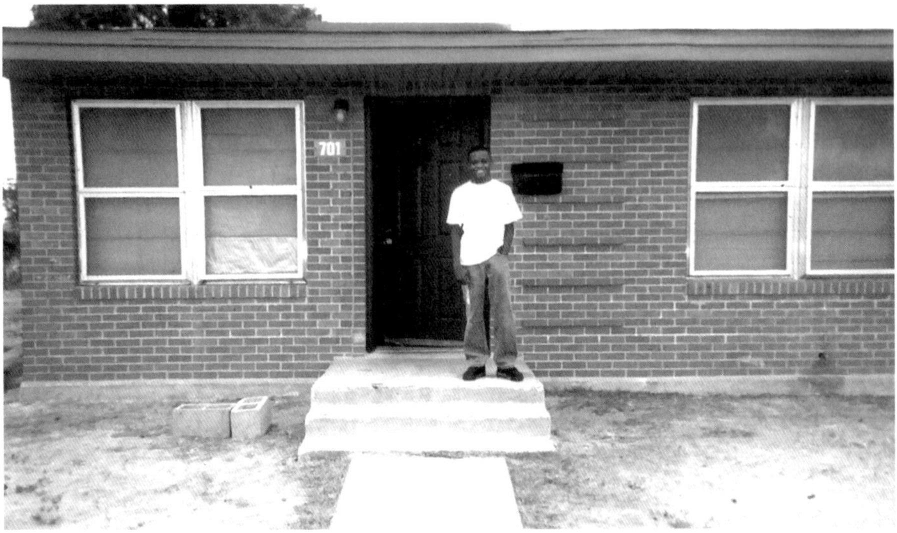

The government housing unit at 701 Rollins Street, pictured here where the youth is standing on the steps, is a former home of the author. Subsidized government housing was considered a step up for many African American families who had only lived in substandard shotgun-style housing. This was the first time many low-income families enjoyed indoor plumbing and other modern conveniences. *Courtesy of Occupants of Unit.*

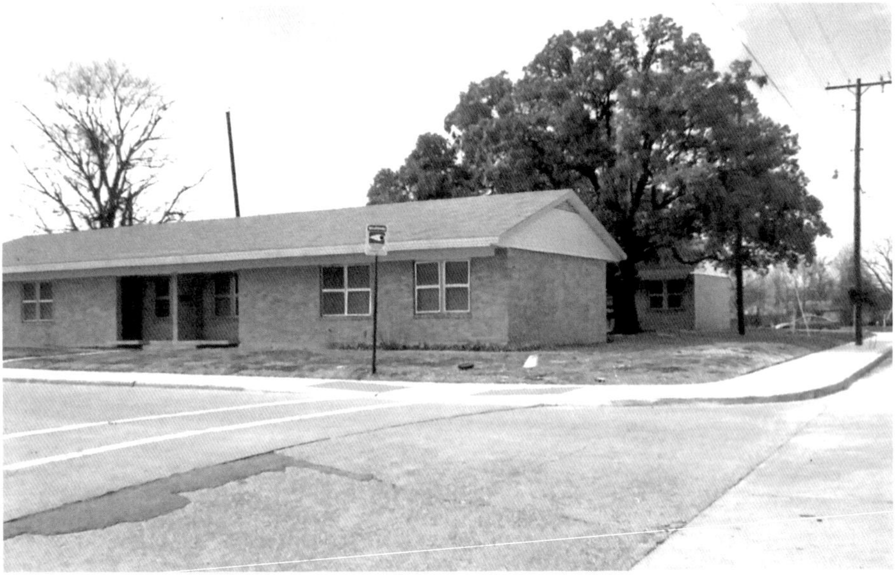

Government subsidized housing on the east side began after the projects were completed on the west side in the 1950s. East side housing was the same style, and many African American families enjoyed modern conveniences. *Courtesy Oswell Person.*

Street, Military Drive and Henderson Street. Again, the projects provided decent housing for many families, who enjoyed, for the first time, life on paved streets, running water and semi-central heating and air conditioning. Over fifty years have passed, and the projects are still meeting the needs of families. The projects provided decent affordable housing; rent payment in the projects was based on an individual's ability to pay, but each family enjoyed the same amenities. On a recent trip to the neighborhood near the east side projects, I noticed that only three shotgun houses are still standing.

CHAPTER SEVEN

HOSPITALS AND MEDICAL CARE

Historically, African American citizens of Bryan had medical doctors but lacked friendly, welcoming hospitals. According to F.G. Anderson's book *The History of Medicine in Brazos County*, Bryan Hospital opened in 1913 and was operated by Dr. W.H. Oliver until 1933. The original building was three stories tall, had twenty-five beds and was near downtown. The hospital closed after Oliver's death and reopened in 1934 under the management of Dr. R.B. Erlinger and Dr. R.B. Grant, who leased it to the Sisters of St. Francis. The Sisters purchased the building in 1936 and renamed the facility St. Joseph Hospital. Today, it is the St. Joseph Regional Medical Center. Dr. H.L. Fountain opened the Fountain Sanitarium in 1908, and according to Anderson, Dr. Albert L. Mondrick developed a hospital in association with his practice in 1913.

In later years, Bryan ISD named the Hammond-Oliver Health Sciences School in honor of Drs. William A. Hammond Sr. and W.H. Oliver. All efforts to open and develop hospitals were private, and there was not a general hospital in Bryan. Understanding again that Bryan was immutably segregated, Dr. William A. Hammond Sr. built a clinic-office where African Americans could readily receive professional consultation and medical attention or service. During this time, there was at least one other African American physician, Arthur E. Thompson, who also served as coach for the Bryan Public School for Colored football team. Prior to the clinic, African Americans were not readily able to get professional and medical services. Although in most cases African Americans were turned away because of their skin color, it is possible they were not served because of their assumed inability to pay. As a result, many minor and even more serious ailments were treated with home remedies.

For example, kerosene mixed with sugar was used to treat the common cold. Kerosene was also used to treat a wound from a rusty nail stick instead of a tetanus shot. Castor oil was another common remedy for colds, along with eating Vick's salve and being rubbed with a product called Penetro. Baking soda and Epsom salt were also common pharmaceuticals used to treat a variety of illnesses. Baking soda was also used for oral hygiene. Sardines, it was thought, would cure mumps when rubbed on the earlobes. Midwives were used in place of obstetricians. Ella Latson, "Old Lady" Calhoun (as she was known), Rachael Cavitt and Minnie Thornton (known as Aunt Minnie) were a few of Bryan's better-known midwives. Minnie Thornton was the aunt of Clifton and James (Jim) Greer, and she delivered both of them, as well as many others. "Old Lady" Calhoun lived on the east side, and when mothers were about to deliver their babies, it was common to hear someone yell,

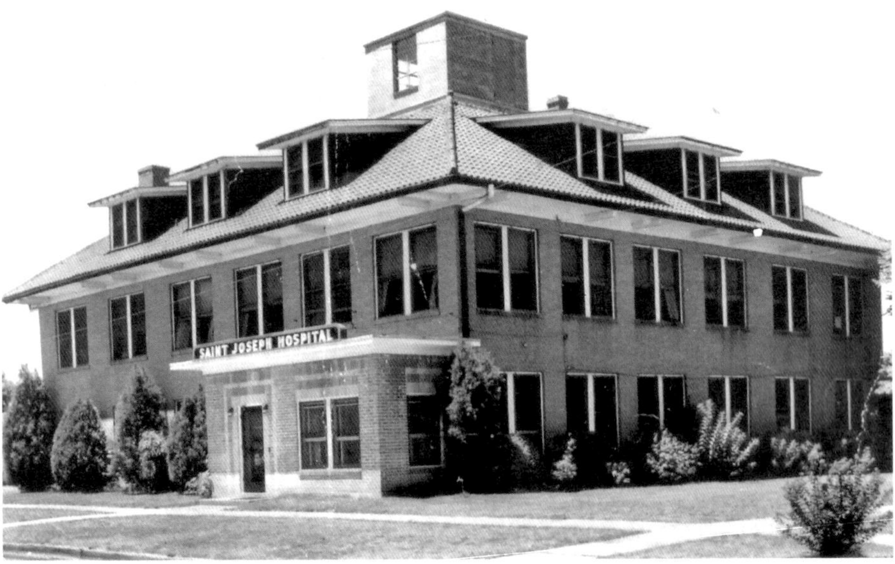

The Bryan Hospital was originally a three-story facility with twenty-five beds. After it was operated by several medical doctors and leased, the Sisters of St. Francis purchased it in 1936 and renamed it St. Joseph. Today, it is called St. Joseph Regional Medical Center. *Courtesy Carnegie Center of Brazos Valley History.*

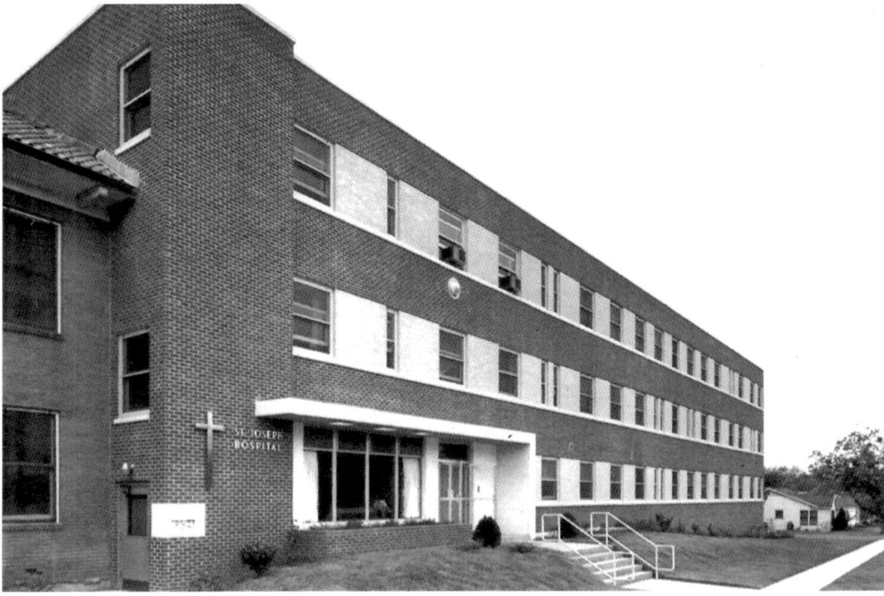

In 1947, because of St. Joseph Hospital's steady expansion, it became necessary to build a Sisters' residence so the Sisters' rooms could be used for patients. In 1953, groundbreaking ceremonies were held and construction began on the hospital's new addition. In 1954, a new three-story wing was completed, thereby adding sixty new beds to the hospital. A brand-new St. Joseph Hospital was built in 1971 at Villa Maria Road at Twenty-ninth Street. *Courtesy Carnegie History Center.*

"Better send for Old Lady Calhoun!" This was during the time when doctors made home visits. After the baby was born, doctors would come and examine both the mother and baby.

In 1928, Brazos County employed an African American nurse to serve "Blacks." She also trained midwives at the Negro Health Center located on the campus of the Bryan Public School for Colored. Dr. William A. Hammond Sr. must have realized the clinic was not adequate for handling serious medical needs. So, in 1929, he opened the sixteen-bed Hammond Memorial Hospital on Randolph and West Seventeenth Streets. According to Brundige, the hospital was "dedicated to suffering humans," and it remained open into the 1950s. Drs. Hammond Sr. and Thompson were joined later by two other physicians, Drs. Samuel J. Sealey and J.M. Franklin. Dr. Sealey practiced medicine in Bryan and Madisonville, Texas, until he and his family moved to Saint Louis, Missouri, in 1950. Sarah Reed owned a convalescent home that was primarily for pregnant women, but it also served ill patients.

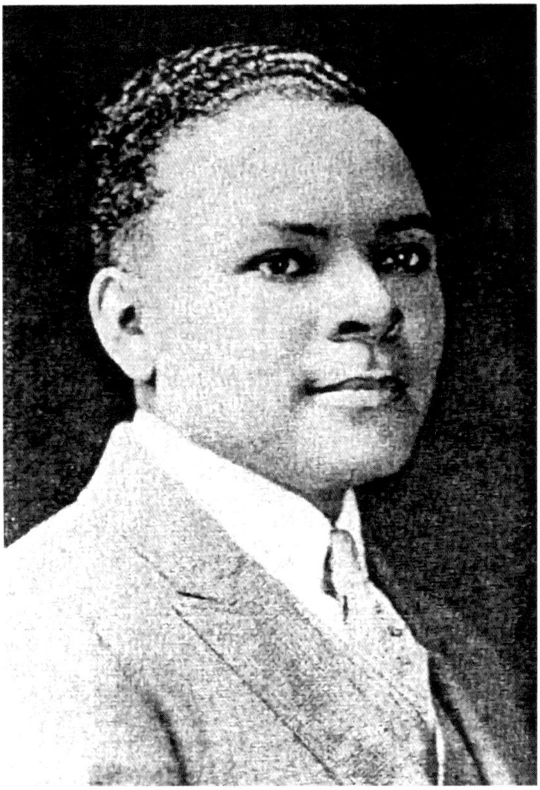

Dr. William A. Hammond Sr. was one of the very early African American surgeons in Bryan, Texas, and perhaps in Brazos County. After graduation from Prairie View A&M College, he earned his medical degree from Meharry Medical College in Nashville, Tennessee, in 1916. He moved to Bryan from his hometown of Hammond, Texas. According to the 1916 graduation catalogue, he and another physician, Dr. Arthur E. Thompson, were classmates. *Courtesy Christyne M. Douglas, Archivist, Meharry Medical College.*

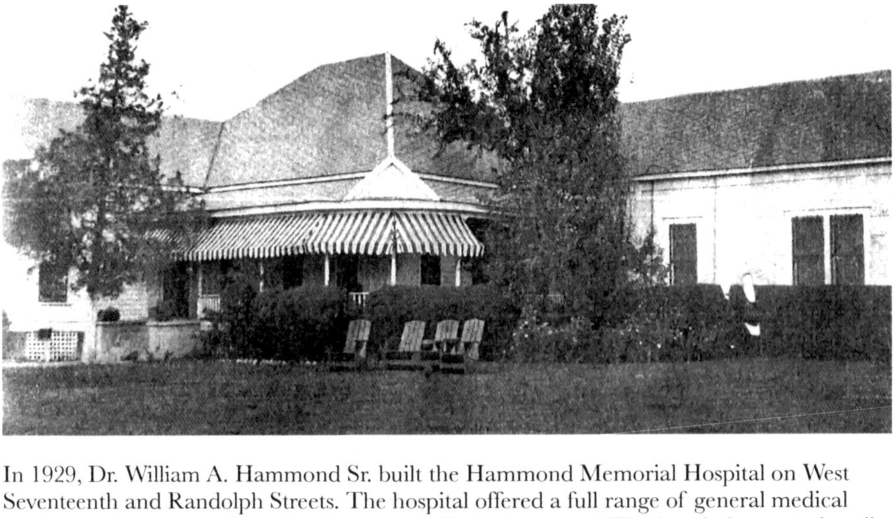

In 1929, Dr. William A. Hammond Sr. built the Hammond Memorial Hospital on West Seventeenth and Randolph Streets. The hospital offered a full range of general medical services and surgery and was "dedicated to suffering humans." The hospital operated until it was demolished in the late 1950s. *Courtesy Carnegie Center of Brazos Valley History.*

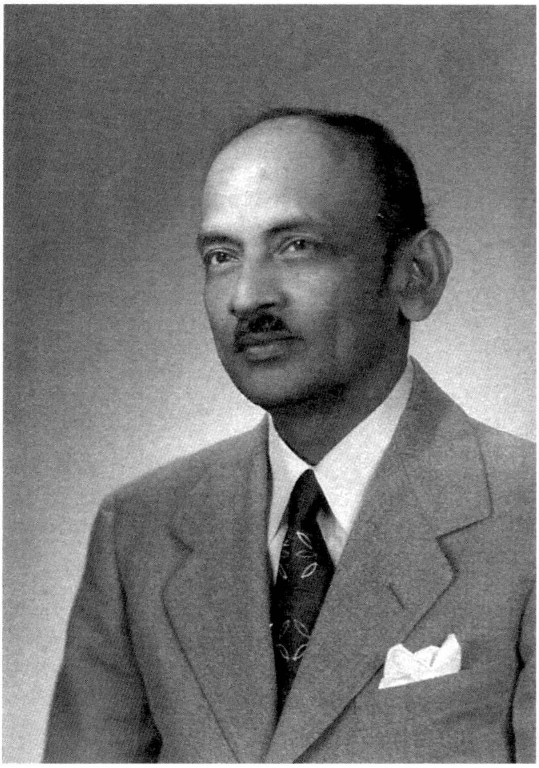

Dr. Samuel J. Sealey Sr. was one of several physicians in Bryan during the late 1930s who graduated from Meharry Medical College. He practiced medicine until 1950, at which time, he and his family moved to Saint Louis, Missouri. His main Bryan office was located downtown on the corner of North Main and Twenty-first Streets. He also traveled to Madisonville to treat patients. His specialty from all accounts was pediatrics, and he was well respected in both communities. *Courtesy Carnegie Center of Brazos Valley History.*

It was located on West Nineteenth Street, not very far from Hammond's hospital, and it was an important partner in the medical services offered to African Americans.

In addition to being a surgeon and owning a clinic and hospital, Hammond was an entrepreneur. He owned rental houses (stated earlier) that provided housing for low-income families, a lumberyard and a kindergarten. He owned a laundry and dry cleaner's that offered both pick-up and delivery service and, as did his other enterprises, provided employment to a number of black families. Dr. Hammond also purchased land for the Grandview Cemetery for African Americans. In addition to all of his contributions, he was involved in civic issues, such as the Negro Chamber of Commerce and PTA.

In spite of a full schedule of civic and professional functions, Dr. and Mrs. William Hammond Sr. were successful parents. They had seven children, six of whom lived. Four daughters and two sons all became professionals. Of the four daughters, Carolyn, whom I interviewed over

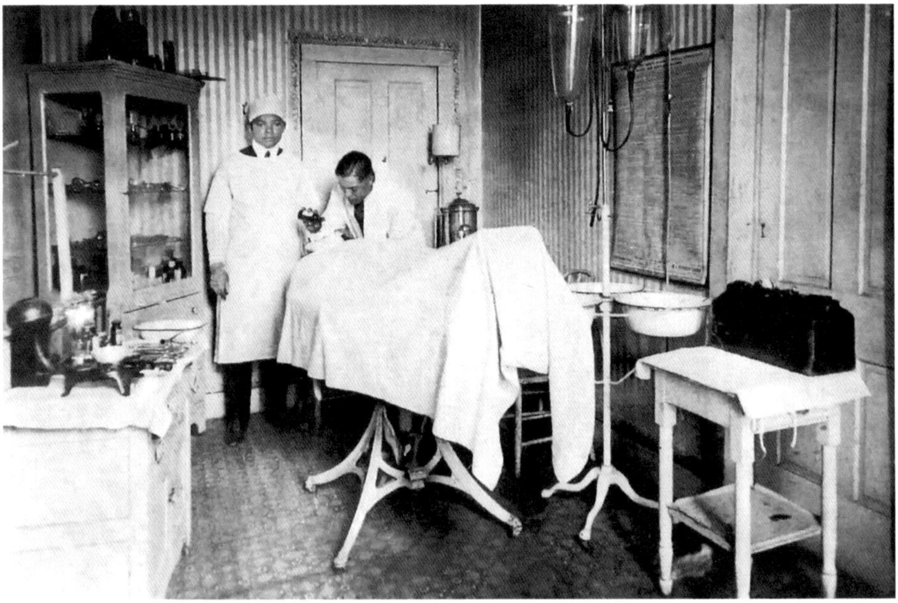

Dr. William A. Hammond Sr. in his hospital operating room with a patient awaiting surgery. Dr. Hammond practiced medicine and performed surgeries in Bryan for many years. He died October 15, 1973. The hospital was in service until it was demolished in the late 1950s. *Courtesy Carnegie Center of Brazos Valley History.*

the phone while doing research for this project, became a physician and is still active. Gladys became an educator, and Prudence became both an educator and a successful businesswoman. Lovie Jewell became a lawyer and returned to Bryan to practice law, possibly the second African American to do so, according to Paul McKay. The older son, William Hammond Jr., became a physician, and the second son, Charles Hammond, became a dentist.

Carolyn now lives in Laurel, Maryland, and her sister Gladys (it is believed) lived in Oklahoma, where she taught school but may have moved to Ohio at some point, which is where Prudence may currently live or may have lived. William A. Hammond Jr. practiced medicine in California, and some of his patients who also moved from Bryan to California were former patients of his father. Charles Hammond lived and practiced dentistry in San Diego.

There were three professional dentists who provided dental care to African Americans: Drs. J.T. Canady, Irving A. Carter and C.W. Flint. Carter and Flint had offices on North Main Street in downtown Bryan.

Dr. Carter took care of E.A. Kemp High School athletes when they received injuries in athletic events that required dental care or surgery. Mrs. Irma Carter, wife of Dr. Carter, taught social studies at Washington Elementary School.

CHAPTER EIGHT

RECREATIONAL ACTIVITIES AND FACILITIES

After-school recreational activities were limited for both boys and girls as there was not a boys' and girls' club in Bryan, although according to the Brazos County Historical Time Line, a YMCA was organized or proposed earlier in the century. As with most things educational and social, some African American teachers made attempts to provide wholesome opportunities where young boys and girls could interact socially in friendly and safe environments when not in school. Oscar Pierce Sr., father of Otis and Oscar Pierce, was a civic- and community-minded parent who established the YAC Club for boys. Many young boys between the ages of twelve and eighteen participated in the YAC Club. There were some evening activities during the week, but on weekends, they filled the days playing sports. Softball and baseball teams were formed, and sportsmanship and teamwork were constant themes for club members.

Claude L. Scurry, the head coach of everything at E.A. Kemp Junior-Senior High School, organized other recreational activities, such as boxing and scouting, as a means of developing character and socialization skills. Most, but not all, participated in the Boy Scouts because some parents could not afford the fees. However, those who did participate—Claude Brown, Herman Brown, James H. Crawford, Charles Murphy and Robert Shields for example—said they enjoyed canoeing and other scout activities. The younger boys, the ones who could afford it, had an opportunity to join the Cub Scouts, and those who did—including Andrew Byrd Jr., Elliott Myers Jr. and Weldon Walton—all said that they enjoyed themselves. Ennis Owens and David Parker exposed young boys to opportunities to develop character, team concepts and skills. They, too, were instrumental in creating a climate for competition in a formal supervised context through sports.

Lula Dean, a day-care owner, opened a house on Fridays and Saturdays as a place for boys and girls to socialize. She allowed them to play a host of games, listen to music and demonstrate their musical talent by playing the piano. Dean insisted that the boys and girls treat each other with respect and demonstrate acceptable social habits and respect for one another. Prudence Hammond Coker, one of Dr. Hammond's daughters, provided young girls with an opportunity to learn proper etiquette and other acceptable social graces. Back then, Bryan did not have a Girl's Inc. or YWCA for young African American females. However, there was a recreational and civic club for young females of Bryan. The club eventually became the Youth Center Club House, and in later years, its name was changed to the Bethune Woman's Club. The club has provided recreational and social opportunities and has also sponsored a variety of activities for young girls, ladies and women. According to *Brazos County History: Rich Past—Bright Future*, Arthur Keats, a teacher, saw the need for teenage recreation and opened a place called Keats' Hall. The hall sponsored various activities. Collie Sanders, a former Kemp student, also opened a place for teenage recreation on Twenty-eighth Street, now called Suncrest Street.

There were other sites, such as Scott's Place and Nelson's Blue Dine Inn, that provided recreational opportunities for young people to congregate and socialize after school and on weekends. Another option for teenagers in Bryan with cars was Smith's Grill, a very popular hangout for teenagers and young adults in neighboring College Station.

In addition to the ones mentioned above, Bob's Confectionery, Walton's Confectionery, Robert Jones' Place and a building next to the Tick Tock Night Club were intended for youth activities. But of all the places for teenage recreation, Knox's Place located on West Nineteenth Street was the most popular. It was owned by Edward H. Knox, a former principal of Washington Elementary School, but it was managed by Searcy Toliver, a World War II veteran. Youth from Bryan as well as the surrounding areas came to Knox's Place to dance to live and jukebox music. Often, after the Friday night athletic events, students would dance to the music played by Kemp High student musicians. E.A. Kemp Junior-Senior High always had talented young musicians, many of whom were tutored first by band director Hardy Murphy and later by Dr. Waymon Webster, who was also a superb musician. Some of the musicians were Lorenzo "Bunny" Scurry, who played in Las Vegas after leaving high school; Fred G. Smith, who played with Ray Charles and arranged for Smokey Robinson; and Sidney Earl Simpson. Another exceptional musician was Marion Jones, who was reportedly accepted in one of the Jazz Lab bands at the University of North Texas (UNT) while still in high school. Donald "Dickie" Childs and James Herman Alberson also attended UNT, and Horace Nelson studied music at Prairie View A&M University. Ennis Green, Charles Watson, Clyde Dove, Albert Griffin, Willie C. Smith and Nathaniel Dove were all student musicians.

All the efforts to provide recreational opportunities for young African Americans were based on individual and group initiatives. One group of individuals, led by Jesse Lee Davenport, formed a gospel singing quartet and called themselves the Utility Gospel Singers. They used to broadcast on the KORA AM station in Bryan. Members of the Gospel Utility Singers included Anise Bell (tenor), Tom Butler, Marvin Cooper (baritone), Zelt Mims, Fred Smith, Charles Sterling (tenor, baritone and one of the lead singers), John L. Williams and Arthur Woodard. They would go from house to house singing and even inspired other African American youths in Bryan to form a doo-wop singing group called The Teekings. Its members were Nat Dove, Rufus Green, Melvin Littleton, Dewayne Mosley and Clinton Walton.

Bryan's African American adults also required entertainment and places in which to socialize, especially since segregation in Bryan's earlier years prevented them from attending white establishments. The January 18, 1906 edition of the *Bryan Daily Eagle* reported, "The old Presbyterian Church has been purchased by C.G. Parsons and is being moved to the west side of town, corner of Clay and Wheelock streets where it will be used as a hall for colored society." Another report from the *Eagle*, dated March 10, 1939, describes how Bryan African Americans established their own social organizations:

> *Feeling that the increasing Negro population is demanding wholesome places of leisure and that a substitute must be offered for places of amusement that often lead to crime. The Negro people have organized to make an effort to have a public library for them here. This Colored Library Association is presenting the Prairie View Dramatic Club in a three-act psychological thriller, "The Hat Mystery," on Wednesday evening at 8:15 in the Kemp high school auditorium.*

In his book *Historic Brazos County*, Robert Borden notes that Dr. I.A. Carter, the aforementioned African American dentist, was elected chairman, and

H.K. Hornsberry (also spelled Harbsberry) served as co-chairman. Other officers included Ellis Johnson, vice-chairman; Mrs. C.E. Cass, secretary; Imogene Sharp, corresponding secretary; I.L. Williams, treasurer; and Reverend T.L. Sanders, chaplain.

Miss Margaret Sims, the city librarian, addressed the third meeting of this library association on March 19, 1939. Again, the *Eagle* reported on this meeting:

> *Many white citizens also attended, among them being James A. Astin, Bryan's new city manager, who made an interesting talk on "Delinquency Reduction Among Colored People." He pointed out that a public library would be an important movement for such a reduction. In his brief address, he also commended the Boy Scout movement among the Negro people, and recommended Girl Scouts, which yet are to be organized.*

The Carnegie Library, built in 1903 with funds donated by Andrew Carnegie, did not serve African Americans, but it opened its doors to all citizens of the community in later years.

A review of the literature on Bryan's parks and recreation revealed much. For example, the City of Bryan did not give serious consideration to organized recreation for citizens until the 1920s. In 1920, city planners purchased 9.5 acres of land for the Sue Haswell Park, and in 1957, a pool with a bathhouse was incorporated into the park structure. However, African American citizens could only watch the white citizens swim in the pool. African American boys swam in the American Legion tank, which was located on Old Kurten Road and Waco Street. The tank also served as the baptismal for the original New Zion Baptist Church. James Allen Graves, who lived on Old Reliance Road (an extension of Pierce Street), had a mud hole deep enough for swimming. Boys who had transportation to the Bryan Air Force Base that was located miles from the city could swim in the integrated pool. Finally, Allen Academy had a pool near its lake, on the property where Henry Williams and his family lived. Although the pool was more like a mud hole with pool-depth designations, my friends and I would trespass and swim during the week, weekends and sometimes at night. But Bryan's African Americans had to wait until about 1957 before they were given a city-operated pool.

In 1946, the city purchased what was called the "Poor Farm," which later became the East Side Addition Park. A headline in a 1956 edition of *Bryan Daily Eagle* read, "Opening programs at Crockett, Bowie and Ben Milam Elementary Schools for whites and at Washington Elementary and E.A. Kemp Junior-Senior High Schools for black children." In 1957, the

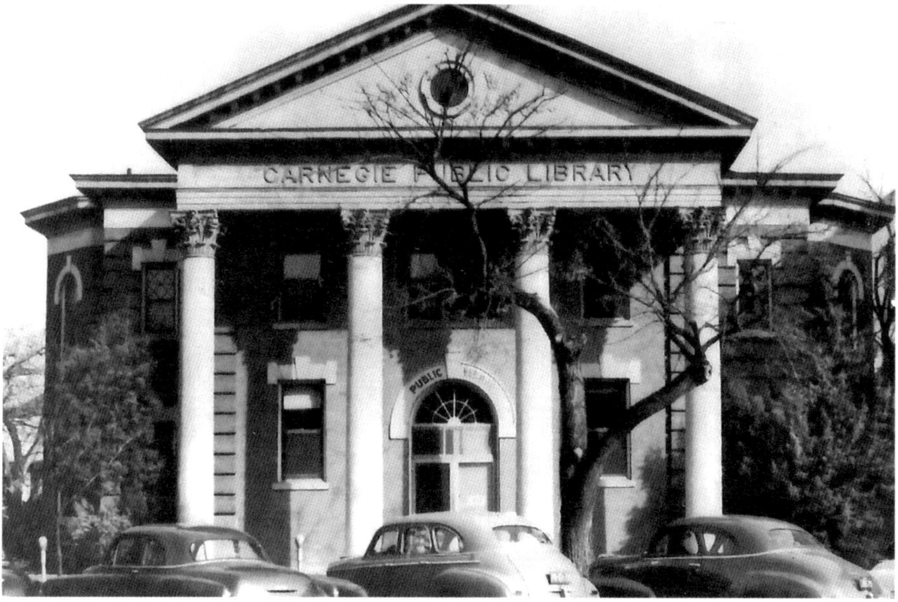

Mr. Andrew Carnegie built ten public libraries in Texas, and of the four currently in existence, the one in Bryan is the oldest. The library opened in 1903 and, in 1999, was renamed the Carnegie Center of Brazos Valley. The name changed again in 2010 to Carnegie History Center. The Bryan City Public Library opened in 1969, and in 2010, the name was changed to Clara B. Mounce Public Library, in honor of its longtime librarian. *Courtesy Carnegie History Center.*

city purchased twenty-three additional lots that were added to the East Side Addition Park and finally opened a public swimming pool for African Americans. A softball field, tennis court and soccer field were also added, as well as two pavilions, ten picnic tables and restrooms. In 1959, the East Side Addition Park was renamed Sadie E. Thomas Memorial Park in honor of Sadie Thomas's contributions to education and recreation. In 1971, Washington Park, which is on the former site of Washington Elementary School, was developed, and it had a basketball court and restrooms. Playground equipment and improved lighting were added later. The oldest park in Bryan, Groves Addition Park, located between Wellington Street and the Southern Railroad, was renamed Claude L. Scurry Park. Williams Park, located on the corner of West Randolph and Twenty-first Streets, was built on the site of the city's first disposal plant and was renamed Neal Park in 1996, in honor of Robert C. Neal. Today, Bryan has three parks named in honor of African Americans. The first recreational center was built in 1998, adjacent to Neal Elementary School.

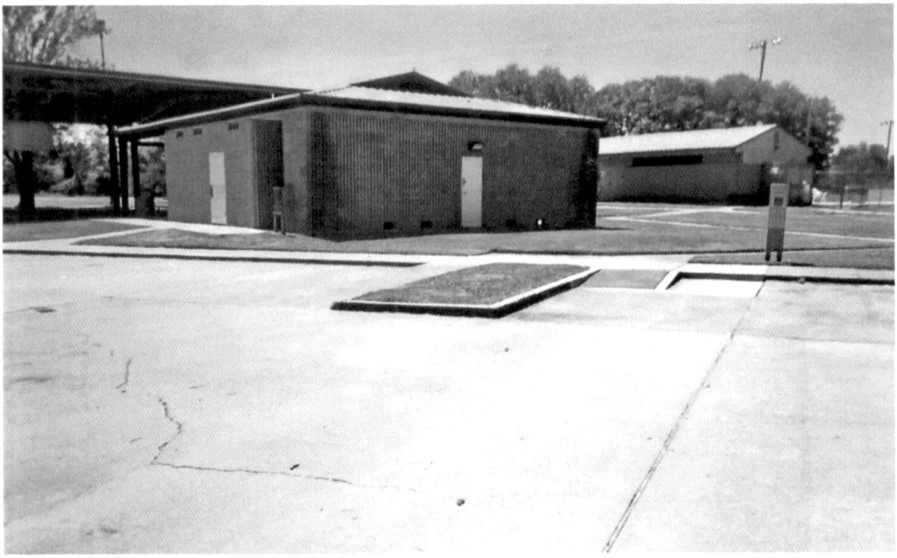

In 1946, the City of Bryan purchased the "Poor Farm," which later became the East Side Addition Park. In 1957, the city purchased twenty-three additional lots that were added to what had become East Side Addition Park. It was at this time that the first modern swimming pool for African Americans was opened. At the same time, a softball field, tennis court, soccer field, two pavilions, ten picnic tables and restrooms were added. *Courtesy Oswell Person.*

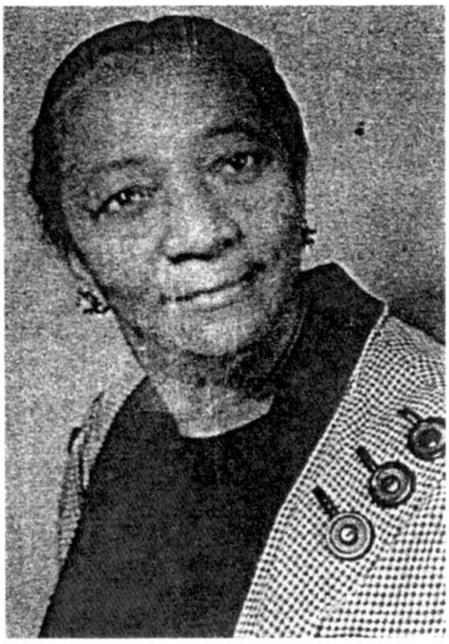

In 1959, the East Side Addition Park, located on what is now Martin Luther King Jr. Street and Moss Street, was renamed Sadie E. Thomas Memorial Park in honor of the contributions to education and recreation Sadie E. Thomas made during her life. Thomas was a venerable English teacher at E.A. Kemp High School for many years. A Texas state historical marker commemorates the long years of service she gave to the African American community. *Courtesy Oswell Person.*

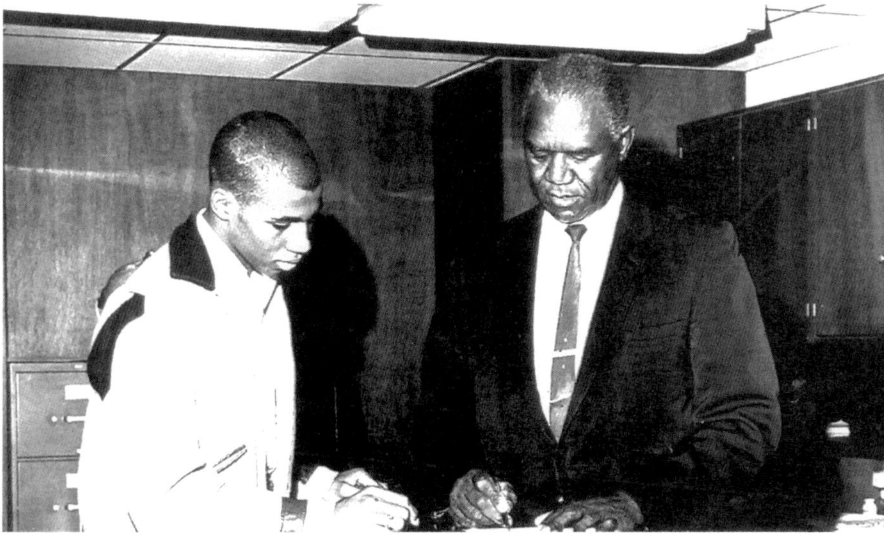

Oak Grove Park was granted to the City of Bryan by Oak Grove's addition developer for use as a city park. County courthouse records from 1913 show a park as part of the city of Bryan. It is the oldest park in Bryan and is located between Wellington Street and the Southern Pacific Railroad. The park was renamed Claude L. Scurry Park. *Courtesy Oswell Person.*

There were four movie theaters in downtown Bryan: the Dixie (which is no longer in operation), Palace, Queen and Starlite. The first three were owned by the Schulmans and were located on Main Street. Presently, the Queen is being restored into a useful landmark. The Starlite Theater owner may have been Clarence Taylor, and the theater was located on the north end of Bryan where the downtown African American businesses were concentrated. Of the three theaters located on Main Street, African Americans were permitted to attend the Palace, but they could only sit in the balcony. Even with restricted seating some of us made it a tribal ritual to attend the midnight shows every Friday night. Seating in the Starlite was unrestricted, and the house was packed every Saturday with boys, who mostly came to see movies starring Buster Crab, Tom Mix, Randolph Scott and Johnny Weissmuller (*Tarzan*). Back in those days, a movie only cost fifteen to twenty-five cents, and one could see the movie repeatedly. The movie *Look Out Sister*, featuring Louis Jordan and Bob Scott, was shown at the Starlite Theater. Scott, if you will recall, had a brother named Kermit Scott who was on the 1930 Bryan Public School for Colored football squad.

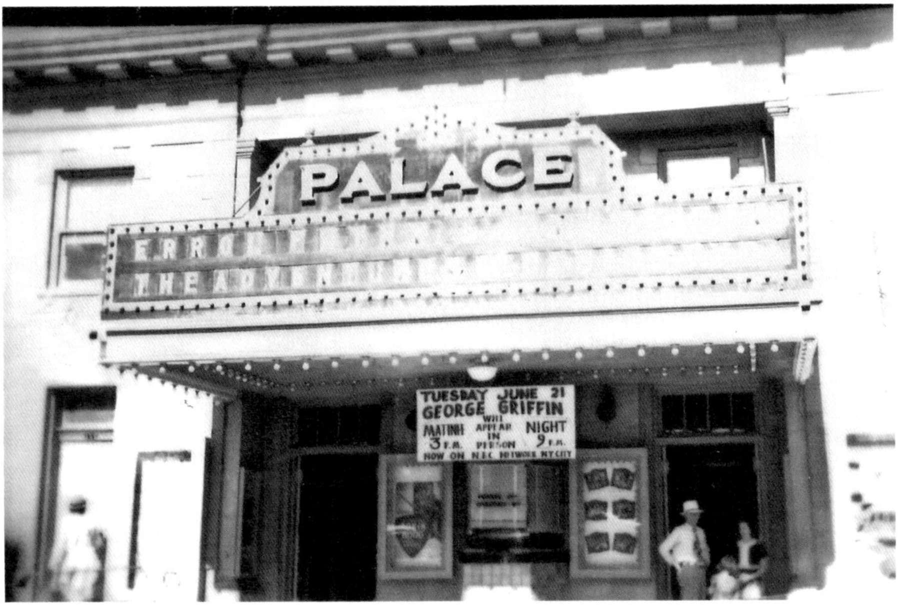

The old Bryan City Hall was purchased and converted into the Palace Theater in 1928. It was one of three theaters owned by Abraham and Morris Schulman and the only one to admit African Americans. In the far left of the photograph, you can see an African American janitor near the entrance designated "colored." *Courtesy Carnegie History Center.*

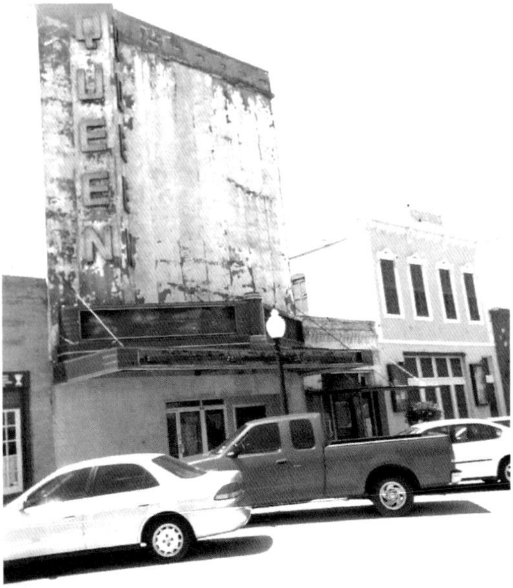

The Queen was one of three theaters owned by Abraham and Morris Schulman. It was rebuilt in 1939 and has the distinction of being the first air-conditioned theater west of the Mississippi River. The Queen is currently being refurbished as a landmark and will be used for offices. The Dixie was the third theater owned by Abraham and Morris Schulman and was also located downtown on South Main Street, not far from the Queen. It has not been in operation for many years. *Courtesy Carnegie History Center.*

Another theater that was perhaps unknown to many citizens was an outdoor sort of makeshift theater located on Pierce Street, just behind the beer joint owned by one of Joe Restivo's sons. Since it was outdoors, it was hard to enjoy the movie and fight mosquitoes at the same time. Another movie theater for African Americans was located on the corner of East Twenty-first and Bradley Streets. The building was later converted into a garage and is still standing at the time of this writing.

CHAPTER NINE

NEWSPAPER AND INFORMATION SOURCES

The *Bryan Daily Eagle* was the primary newspaper for citizens of Bryan, Texas, for years. The paper, as I recall, was not hospitable in its coverage of African American citizens. For the most part, it reported unflattering stories about murders and vandalism, and such information and news demeaned and maligned citizens of color. Eventually the *Eagle*'s coverage changed, and articles took on a more positive slant. However, in the meantime, if African Americans wanted news and other information, they had to import it from outside of Bryan. Two newspapers that carried stories with positive images and information about African Americans were the *Chicago Defender* and *Pittsburgh Courier*. James T. Murphy (who was often referred to as J.T.) was the contact and distributor for the *Chicago Defender*, and I was the local contact for the *Pittsburgh Courier*. We received and delivered these papers to our respective customers. J.T. had a fairly large customer base, which he successfully maintained for several years. My customer base was quite small and not maintained very long. As I recall, an adult named Otis Johnson who lived in Freedmen Town was the contact and distributor for another imported paper, the name of which I have forgotten. Fred Hickman's father distributed the *Bryan Daily Eagle* to the African American sides of town.

For a period of time, Reverend C.C. Jammer, pastor of Lee Chapel Methodist Church, published *TREND Magazine*. Perhaps it was intended to fill gaps left by the *Eagle*. The *TREND* provided local news about communities in Bryan and Brazos County. I remember only reading two articles from this magazine. One was about Billy Ray Smith, who was a student at Lincoln

University in Pennsylvania at the time; the other was an article about my 1959 tour of navy duty in Hawaii.

The radio was another source of information. Commentators Gabriel Heater and Paul Harvey were two radio personalities I remember fairly well, and we could always get news and information, accurate or not, from the local barbershop and beauty shop. Individuals who could afford subscriptions to *Ebony*, *Jet* and *Sepia* were aware and exposed to news and information about the world on a much broader scale. These magazines featured national, and sometimes international, news about people of color. Consequently, they were sources of pride in the community. Often, when new magazines were received, the discarded ones were read by neighbors who could not afford paid subscriptions. In addition to *Ebony*, *Jet* and *Sepia* subscriptions, a limited number of individuals who were members of the National Association for the Advancement of Colored People (NAACP) received the official magazine *CRISIS*. Perhaps an even smaller number of individuals purchased *Look*, *Reader's Digest* and the *Saturday Evening Post*. Parents of classmates or neighbors who worked out of town, namely in Dallas and Houston, would bring old copies of the *Dallas Morning News* and the *Houston Chronicle* home, thereby providing locals an opportunity to read about events, people and places beyond Bryan, Texas.

CHAPTER TEN
CITY TRANSPORTATION

According to the Handbook of Texas Online, the population of Bryan had reached 4,132 by 1910. This growth in population caused the city to build an interurban railroad to College Station. The interurban railroad operated until the 1920s, when it was replaced by bus service. (Incidentally, the literature review did not reveal an ongoing history of city bus service after the 1920s.)

There was, however, a bus service that operated during the 1950s, though I am not sure if it was city or private. The bus provided transportation to and from the east and west sides and to College Station. It was the principal mode of transportation for citizens without private vehicles. The designated bus routes were along the three main arteries in the African American neighborhoods: Pierce, East and West Nineteenth Streets and West San Jacinto Highway. The transfer point for inter-city and College Station was downtown on Twenty-sixth Street. Limiting bus routes to Pierce, Nineteenth Streets and San Jacinto Highway meant patrons had to walk considerable distances to catch the bus. Patrons who lived on the far end of Waco Street and Pierce Street's extension had a rather long walk to the Pierce Street bus stop. The same was true for customers who lived at the far end of West Fifteenth, Sixteenth and Seventeenth Streets. In addition to walking from home to the bus stop, domestic workers (women mostly) had to walk to their places of work after they got off the bus. This same trek was repeated for individuals after a long workday.

Another limitation of the bus service was its hours of operation. It operated from about 7:00 a.m. to 10:00 p.m., Monday through Saturday,

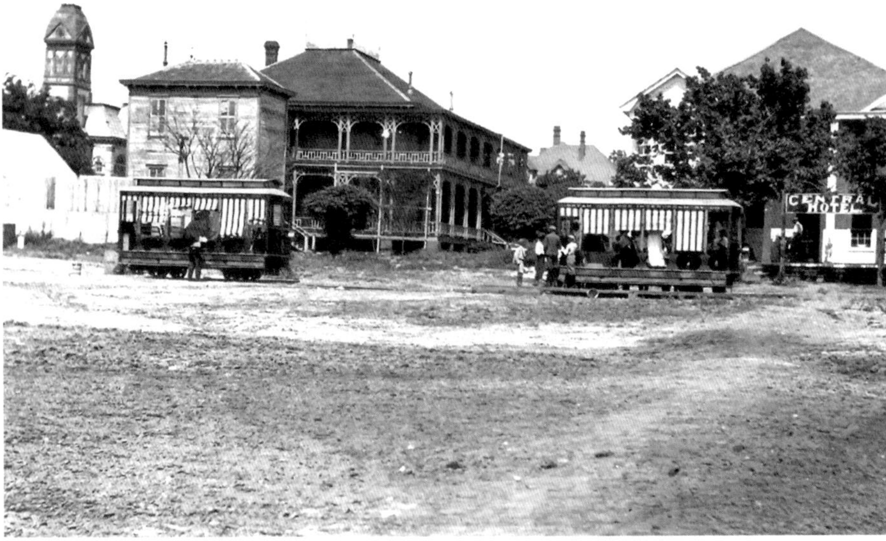

In 1910, the population of the city of Bryan grew to over 4,100, which prompted the city to build an interurban railroad to neighboring College Station. The interurban railroad operated until the 1920s. In the 1950s, Bryan had a bus service that provided transportation from Bryan to College Station. *Courtesy Carnegie History Center.*

and the Saturday hours may have been shorter. Citizens whose workday began before 7:00 a.m. were not served by bus transportation, and neither were patrons who worked until after 10:00 p.m. (mostly café employees, my aunt included). Those who worked nights at Texas A&M University's Memorial Student Center Bowling Alley were also affected by restricted bus hours. Patrons coming from their jobs at night, again, had to walk from downtown to their individual communities. Such walks for some were quite a distance. The limited bus routes, schedules and hours of operation were most burdensome and not compatible with customer needs. On a more positive note, while having to walk rather long distances to catch the bus was an inconvenience, those who did realized great health benefits.

CHAPTER ELEVEN

ELECTED OFFICIALS

Strides Forward

Fear the man who feels himself a slave. He'll want to make a slave of you.
—*John Holt,* Freedom and Beyond

While Brazos County had elected African American officials, Bryan did not have a sustained line of elected city officials until 1968. According to Paul McKay, Brazos County elected Dennis B. Ballard to the commissioners' court seven times from 1880 to 1904. McKay also notes that another black man, H.M. Maddox, joined Ballard on the commissioners' court in 1888. In addition to Commissioners Ballard and Maddox, an African American named Elias Mays represented Brazos County in the Texas Legislature in 1879 and 1889. In the 1880s, Willis van Hook was a Bryan city alderman, the title used for commissioners before 1917. But on July 28, 1968, seventy-nine years after the date listed for elected and appointed officials, Pat Lester, staff writer for the *Eagle*, wrote an article entitled "First Negro to Hold Office." Harmon "Son" Bell was elected as a Bryan city commissioner and served from July 23, 1968, to April 13, 1971, and a second time from August 29, 1972, to April 27, 1976. Bell served as mayor pro tem from April 8, 1969, to April 13, 1971. The title city commission was changed to city council on April 10, 1973. As Bell was leaving the council for a second time, Ples Turner joined the council and stayed on it for ten years. Other African Americans who have been elected to the council are Edward L. Aycox, Paul Madison Sr. and Annette Stephney, who was the first African American female to serve as mayor pro tem. Two men of color, Richard

M. Cortez Sr. and Paul Madison, are listed in the city's directory as council members representing single Districts 1 and 2, respectively. Data sources for the 1880s on elected African American officials, while incomplete, indicate city titles for elected officials between the years 1880 and 1917 changed from alderman to commission manager and changed again in 1973 to its present title of councilman.

THE NEGRO BUSINESS LEAGUE, NAACP AND NEGRO CHAMBER OF COMMERCE

In 1918, the year the Bryan NAACP branch was founded, a group of African Americans met to form a local branch of the Negro Business League. They met at White and Thompson Drug Store, which was located in downtown Bryan at 2311 North Main Street. Present in the group were F.D. Vaughn Jr., Drs. William A. Hammond Sr. and A.E. Thompson, C.W. Flint, W.M. Harrison, C.E. Lewis, W.E. Pigford, N.D. White, Ed Scott, Reverend S.E. Diggs, J.T. Cooper, O.E. Meador and I.N. White. Men not present were Reverends U.S. Keeling, L.J. Jackson and W.H Jackson and another man named T.W. Phillips. Professor O.E. Meador and I.N. White were selected as chairman and secretary pro tem, respectively. The body unanimously elected the aforementioned temporary officers as regular officers for the year. Other officers elected were Dr. A.E. Thompson, first vice-president; N.D. White, second vice-president; Dr. C.W. Flint, assistant secretary; W.E. Pigford, treasurer; W.M. Harrison, assistant treasurer; and Ed Scott, chaplain.

In addition to the Colored Library Association, African Americans organized the first chapter of the NAACP in 1919 and the Negro Chamber of Commerce in 1928. An article in the April 30, 1919 edition of the *Eagle* reported:

> *On Sunday afternoon the Colored people of Bryan and Brazos County met at the New Chapel Baptist Church for the purpose of forming a branch organization of the National Association for the Advancement of Colored People (NAACP) for Bryan and Brazos County. Reverend S.E. Diggs, acting as master of ceremony, called the meeting to order, after which the purpose of the meeting was explained by I.N. White. The matter was fully*

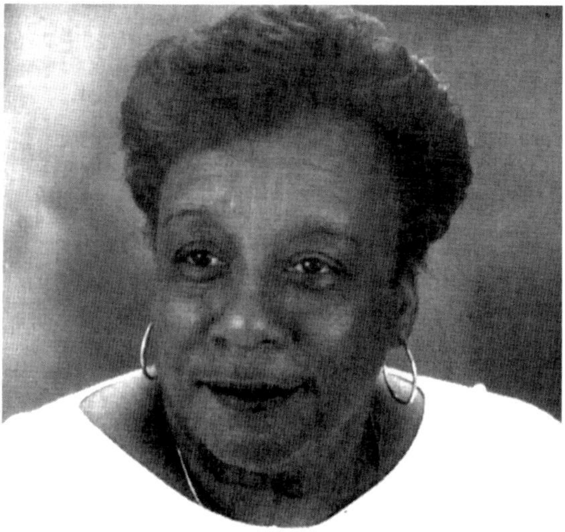

Annette Idlebird Stephney was the first African American female to serve on the Bryan City Council and as mayor pro tem. Mrs. Stephney died October 28, 2009. *Courtesy All School Reunion 2000.*

> *discussed by all present and it was definitely decided to organize a branch of the national association.*

The article explained that individuals joining the newly formed organization paid one dollar or more for membership. A second meeting was held on May 5, 1919, at Shiloh Baptist Church. I.N. White, the first NAACP president, published an eloquent and tactful article in the *Eagle* in October 1919. His article was labeled as an advertisement for the NAACP because it commented on several front-page articles on racial violence in Arkansas, Nebraska and Texas that had appeared in the fall of 1919. In the article, White attempted to ease any fear and suspicion of local African Americans and the newly organized NAACP:

> *As to the history of Bryan for the past of years that I have lived here, it has been, for the most part, very, very commendable indeed in respect to general conditions affecting relations of the races. Bryan and Brazos County enjoy a record to be envied by every county surrounding, and for that matter, the great commonwealth of Texas must with pride point to the record of this county and boast of the race conduct of this child it's raising, while many of the more prosperous centers, richer by endowment and more attractive by popular bequest, have been writhing in turmoil, blood and great sin to the*

> *utter shame and disgrace of the parent mother Texas. In the meanwhile, we, the citizenry of this county, have looked on with awe-stricken eyes, shuddered with dismay, and have hidden our faces in skies effaced by lawless practices. We take pride in the thought that, should Texas be called upon by civilization to present proof of her better self, Brazos County would be her best offering "en sample" for inspection, and I dare say it would inevitably be chosen. This does not mean to condone crime and whatever of injustices that may have been measured to members of either race; for Brazos County, like a child of a household, is guilty of mistakes and wrongs and has strayed at times from the teaching of its mother evinced in her constitutional precepts. But she has never permitted herself to wander so far away from the path of rectitude that she failed to hear the pleas of her broken-hearted mother, the constitution, and heed the call to return to sane and equitable methods of procedure...The Colored people have no secrets to withhold. Their organizations are as wide open for inspections as their churches. In fact, inspection is what they prefer... We ask for more encouragement and less distrust...Our consciences are unfettered and our motives as pure as in the days when the serenity of peace possessed.*

The Negro Chamber of Commerce was another organization formed by African Americans in Bryan. It was headed by William A. Hammond Sr., the medical doctor who founded the only hospital for African Americans in Bryan. According to a May 6, 1929 article in the *Eagle*, it was largely through the activities of the "Negro Chamber of Commerce in Bryan that sufficient funds were made available to secure full time services of the Negro Nurse, Miss Ethel Butler in Brazos County. The good work she is doing here is convincing evidence of the need for public health work among the Negro."

In the same article were names of the chamber members, headed by Dr. William A. Hammond; physicians A.E. Thompson and J.M. Franklin; dentists I.A. Carter and P.R. Johnson; E.A. Kemp Junior-Senior High principal R.C. Neal (who was also assistant principal of the Bryan Public School for Colored); and teachers Fannie Diggs, Sadie Thomas, Lola Sadberry, Juanita Martinez, Mary Keatts and Ada Hall. Ministers J.W. Rhodes, S.E. Diggs, L.A. Greenwood, E.M. Griggs (who was also superintendent of the Bryan Orphan Home), O.H. Bean, E.C. Ransom, R.L. Sadberry, G. O'Neil and J.E. Smith were also members of the chamber.

Other members included Ethel Butler, who was a county health nurse; H.K. Hornsberry, the county's agricultural agent and also co-chairman of the Colored Library Association; F.D. Benson; F. Osborne; George Wiley;

John Lev Thomas, who worked in life insurance; Josh Green, who was a fraternal insurance agent; J.H. Anderson, who was a fraternal insurance agent and a farmer; and A.S. Keatts, who was both a real estate and fraternal insurance agent. Farmers Heslip, John Sadberry, Earnest Sheets, M.S. Bradley, Joe Tiggs and Charles Hays were also part of the chamber, as were grocery merchants Arthur Neal and C.G. McGowan; paving contractor Fred Martinez; shoemaker A.B. Evans; builders and contractors John Jackson, Tom Siler and Walter Brown; and garage operator Marion Payne. Still other chamber members were café owners William Harrison; hotel owner Tommie Turner; tailors Joe Cooper and Earnest Cass; barbers R.B. Goosby, Henry Crawford, H.C. Mosley and William R. McQueen; Henry Jenkins; porter Bremond Triggs; and cabinetmaker Jethro Hatchett.

BRYAN CITY OFFICIALS IN 2019:

Isaac Butler, Jr., Constable, Precinct 4, Elected 1996-
Prentiss Madison, Councilman, Single Member District 2, Elected 2016-

BRAZOS COUNTY OFFICIALS IN 2019:

Irma Cauley, Commissioner, Precinct 4, Elected 2010-
Jarvis Parsons, District Attorney,Elected 2012-

PAST BRAZOS COUNTY OFFICIALS:

Rose Jones, Justice of Peace, Precinct 4, Elected 2010, served until 2015
Carey Cauley, Commissioner, Precinct 4, Elected 1995, served until 2009
Milton Turner, Commissioner, Precinct 4, served until 1994

CHAPTER TWELVE

PRINCIPALS, TEACHERS AND STAFF

From 1885 to 1930, the principals of Bryan Public School for Colored were A.H. Colwell, Paul Landry, Elijah Alonzo Kemp and Robert C. Neal. From 1931 to 1961, the principals of E.A. Kemp Junior-Senior High School were Robert C. Neal and Colquitt D. Yancy. From 1931 to 1970, the principals of Washington Elementary School were Lon Nash, Edward H. Knox Sr., Thomas W. Cole Sr. and Oliver Wayne Sadberry Sr.

Pictures of A.H. Colwell and Pal (Paul) Landry, the first two principals of Bryan Public School for Colored, were not available, nor were pictures of Lon A. Nash and Thomas W. Cole Sr. But pictures of all succeeding principals are included on the following pages.

Elijah Alonzo Kemp and Robert C. Neal served as the third and fourth principals of Bryan Public School for Colored. R.C. Neal was the assistant principal and became principal after the death of Kemp in 1929. He was also principal of the new E.A. Kemp Junior-Senior High for the years 1930–1958. He was followed by Colquitt D. Yancy.

When E.A. Kemp Junior-Senior High opened, the former Bryan Public School for Colored was renamed Washington Elementary School in 1931. Lon Nash was principal of the newly named school, followed by Edward H. Knox Sr., who served from 1934 to 1943. He was followed by Thomas W. Cole Sr. Oliver Wayne Sadberry Sr. became principal in 1949 and served until 1970. In 1949, George Washington Carver Elementary School was built on the west side, and the first principal was Colquitt D. Yancy. He was followed by Otha Byrd.

The first principal of the new E.A. Kemp Senior High School was Colquitt D. Yancy, and Claude L. Scurry was his assistant principal. Yancy was followed by W.D. Dunn, and the assistant principal was James Rose. After the new senior high school was built, the former E.A. Kemp Junior-Senior was renamed R.C. Neal Junior High. The principals of Neal Junior High were Ulysses S. Morgan, Dr. Wendell Davis Jr. and Claude L. Scurry, who was the last principal before the schools were desegregated in 1971. Gregg Travillion was the last African American principal at George Washington Carver Elementary School before it closed in 1971. The school became Carver-Kemp Campus, and Paul Kunz was principal from 1971 to 1988.

Great care and effort was taken to confirm and recall all the dedicated and devoted principals and teachers who helped educate generations of African American boys and girls between the years 1885 and 1971. However, some names could not be found, but many were part of the Bryan Public School for Colored, E.A. Kemp Junior-Senior and the Senior High Schools. Others were part of Washington and George Washington Carver Elementary Schools. Still others were a part of all the schools for African Americans, until Brazos County schools were desegregated. Together, they provided hundreds and hundreds of combined years of service to the community. It was not uncommon to find individuals whose careers in education spanned thirty to forty-five years in the classroom or a combination of classroom and school administration.

The principals of Bryan Public School for Colored between the years 1885 and 1930 and those of Washington Elementary Schools between 1931 and 1970, as stated earlier, were A.H. Colwell, Paul Landry, Elijah Alonzo Kemp, Robert C. Neal, Lon A. Nash, Edward H. Knox, Thomas W. Cole Sr. and Oliver Wayne Sadberry Sr. Some of the teachers were Anne Alberson, Pearl Brooks, Mamie Burrows, Lucille Byrd, Beatrice Calhoun, Lula Callier, Irma Carter, Corrine Cass, (Mrs.) Dickson, Fannie Diggs (also Fairview School principal), Ada Ford, Lenora Green, Ella Mae Gregg, Leila Hall, Ada Scott Hall, Juanita Cunningham Hunter, Hattie Jackson, Vernell Jackson (not related), Mary Keatts, Carrie King, Eloise King, (Mrs.) Oliphant and Lawrence King, Juanita Martinez, Sylvia McIntosh, Lelia Nash, Willie Lee Neal (wife of Robert C. Neal), Atoy Peterson, James Phillips, Johnnie L. Pillows, Lorraine Ocheltree, Cornelia Reed, Neal Reed, Lola Sadberry, Doris Scurry, Clara Smith, Annie Stoval, (Mrs.) Tates, Mabel Thomas, Geraldine Toliver and Jessie Mae Walton. E.J. Noble was the school custodian.

In 1931, Bryan Public School for Colored was named E.A. Kemp Junior-Senior High School, and in 1961, a new E.A. Kemp Senior High was built.

Principals, Teachers and Staff

Here is a list of teachers who taught at these schools between the years 1931 and 1960 and 1961 and 1971:

E.A. Kemp Junior-Senior High School

Myrtle Allen

Louise Anderson

Edward Aycox

Lennie Bailey

Olivia Banks

Fred D. Batts (former principal of John M. Moore)

Margaret Bell

Samuel C. Brisco

Ellen Buttrill

Richard Calhoun

Minnie Clopton

Rose M. Cowan

Hazel Daily

Robert Guyden

Ruby L. Handcox

Betty J.D. Hatchett

Marion Haynes

Jimmy Herron

Loma Hodges

James Johnson

Troy Johnson

Willa E. Johnson

Major Jones

Irene Lane

Edessie McClendon

Bryan Public School for Colored

Anne Orabel Alberson

Mamie Burrows

Lucille Byrd

Beatrice Calhoun

Lula Callier

Irma Carter

Corrine Cass

Winston T. Cole Sr.

A.H. Colwell

Ada Ford

Lenora Green

Ella M. Gregg

Ada Scott Hall

Lelia Hall

Juanita Cunningham Hunter

Hattie Jackson

Vernell Jackson

Mary Keatts

Elijah A. Kemp

Carrie King

Lawrence King

Edward H. Knox Sr.

Paul Landry

Juanita Martinez

Lelia Nash

E.A. Kemp Junior-Senior High School

Willie Moore Jr.

Hardy Ray Murphy

Willie Lee Neal

A.K. O'Neal

Royce Pace

William Portis

Adolphus R. Price

Mel Pruitt

Freddie Mae Robinson

Claude L. Scurry

Imogene Sharp

Charles A. Shead

Alma H. Simmons

Delores Stubberfield

Edna Erle Tarrow

Cora H. Tennant

Lloyd Thomas

Sadie E. Thomas

Hiawatha Webber

Bernice Webster

Waymon Webster

Robert Wilson

Cecil Wooley

Johnnie L. Wyatt

Dolores Yancy (wife of Colquitt Yancy)

Bryan Public School for Colored

Lon Nash

Willie Neal

Lorraine Ocheltree

Mrs. Oliphant (first name unknown)

Atoy Peterson

James Phillips

Willie Pruitt

Cornelia Reed

Neal Reed

Lola Sadberry

Oliver W. Sadberry Sr.

Doris Scurry

Clara Smith

Annie Stoval

Mabel Thomas

Geraldine Toliver

Jessie M. Walton

Sylvia Sadberry worked as a secretary at one of the schools. Walter Carr, Johnny Damon and Henry Sims were custodians, and Johnnie M. Jackson and Elizabeth Sterling were part of the lunchroom staff.

In 1949, George Washington Carver Elementary School opened, and between the years 1949 and 1971, the principals were Colquitt D. Yancy and Otha Byrd, and William G. Hall was assistant principal. Some of the teachers were Estelle Adams, Anne Orabel Alberson, Shirley Birdsong, Ethel Miller Cafeteria, Inez Daniel, Annie Mae Grays, Inez Grays, Vernell Jackson, Katie Johnson, Mabel Knox, Lila Lane, Teresa Love, Ethel Morgan, Willie Lee Neal, Blossie T. Phillips, Doris Scurry, Maggie Sheppard, Ethel Shipmon, Eudora Smith, Mazie Nell Smith, Anne Sterling, Dolores Stubberfield, George Vaults, Tommie Williams and Dolores Yancy.

After E.A. Kemp Senior High School opened in 1961, E.A. Kemp Junior-Senior High became R.C. Neal Junior High School. The principals from 1961 to 1971 were Ulysses S. Morgan, Dr. Wendell Davis Jr. and Claude L. Scurry. Some of the teachers and staff were

Mrs. Anne Alberson (English)
Mrs. Linnie Bailey (art)
Mrs. Ellen Buttrill (reading)
Mr. Carey Cauley (history)
Mrs. Myrtle Crosby (music)
Mr. Iney C. Cunningham (science)
Mrs. Inez Grays (special education)
Mrs. Laura Jackson (PE)
Mr. Vernell Jackson (coach)
Mrs. Willa Johnson (home economics)
Mrs. Lila Mae Lane (math)
Miss Lollie Marshall (school nurse)
Mrs. Lorraine Ocheltree (English)
Mr. Bobby Joe Perry (coach)
Mrs. Effie A. Perry (math)
Mrs. M. Sanders (math)
Mrs. P. Sewell (reading)
Mr. C.A. Shead (band)
Mr. Lloyd Thomas (agriculture)
Mr. Elvin Tyrone (world geography)
Mrs. Ora Waldron (English)
Mr. John Watkins (math)
Mrs. Gloria White (school secretary)
Mrs. E. Wilson (school librarian)

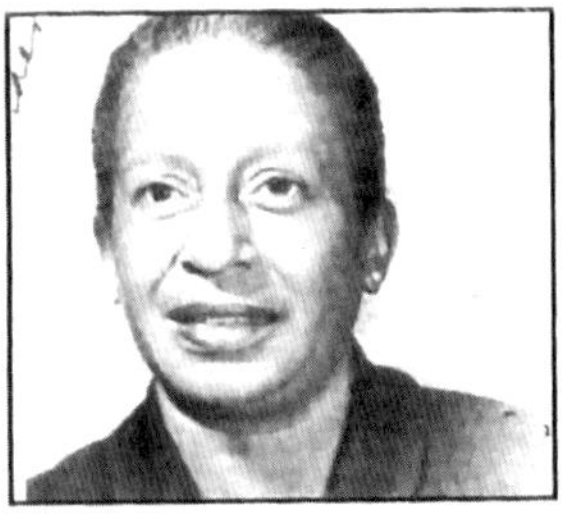

Mrs. Louise Anderson

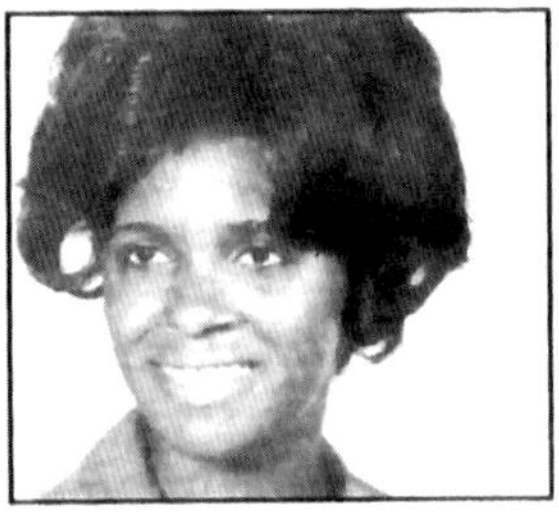

Mrs. Lennis Bailey

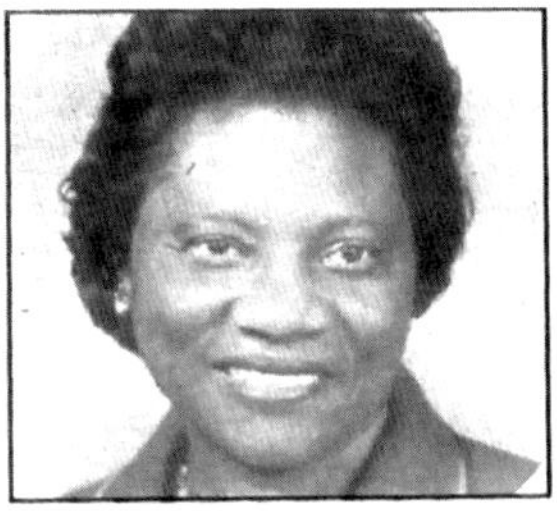

Mrs. Olivia Banks

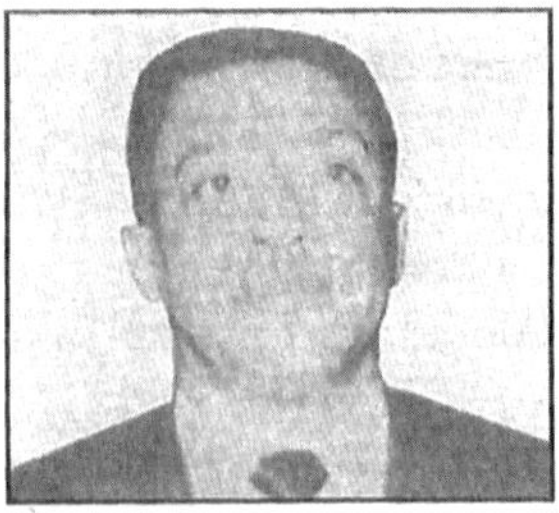

Mr. Otha Byrd
George Washington Carver

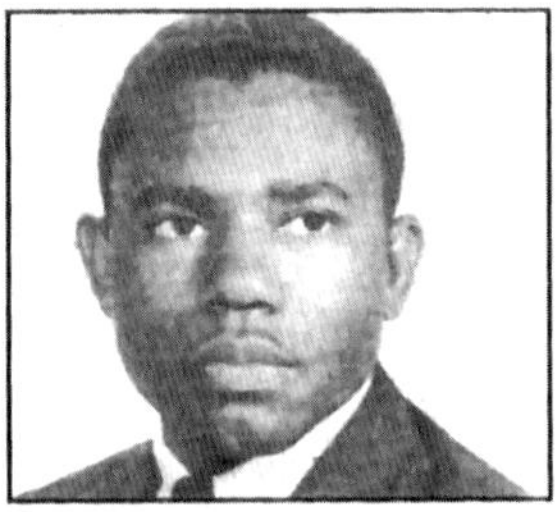

Mr. Richard Calhoun

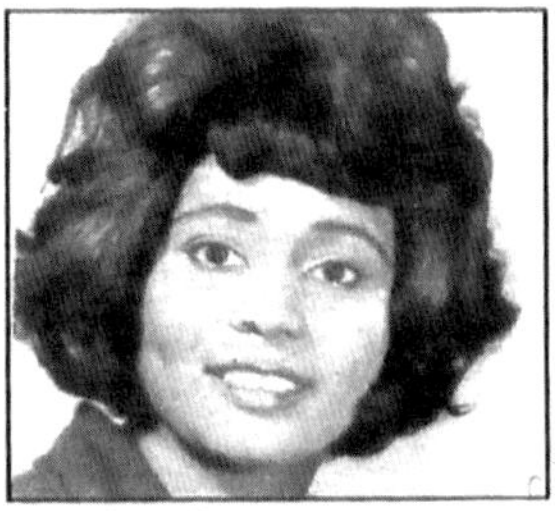

Mrs. Rose Cowan

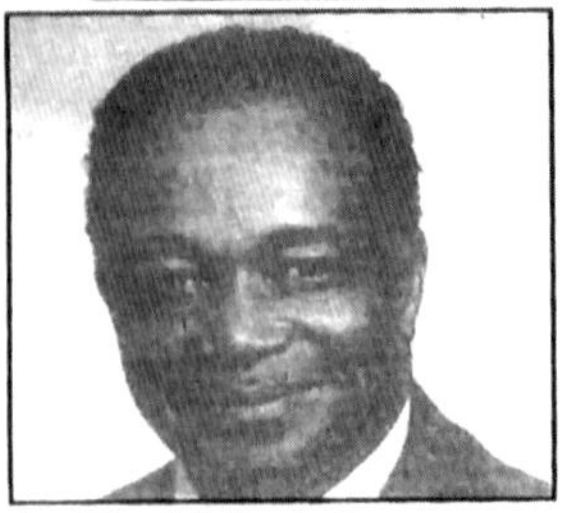

Dr. Wendell Davis, Jr.
Second Principal of R. C. Junior High School

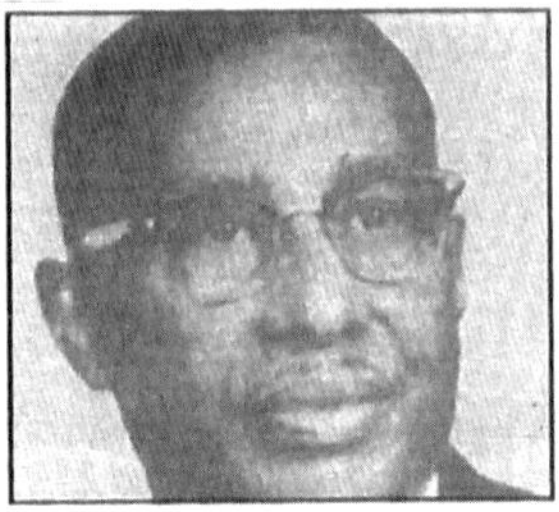

Mr. W. D. Dunn
E. A. Kemp Senior High

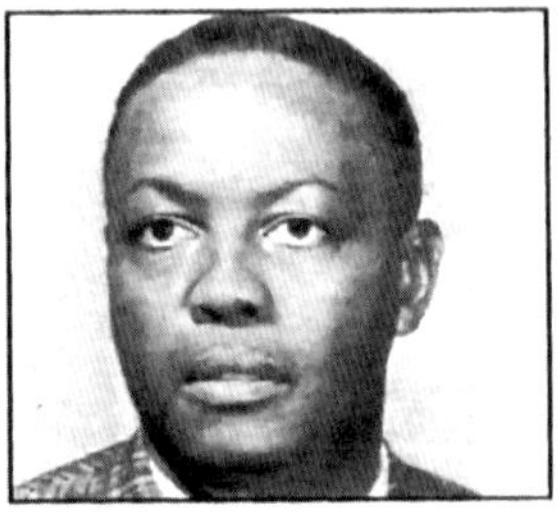

Mr. Robert Guyden

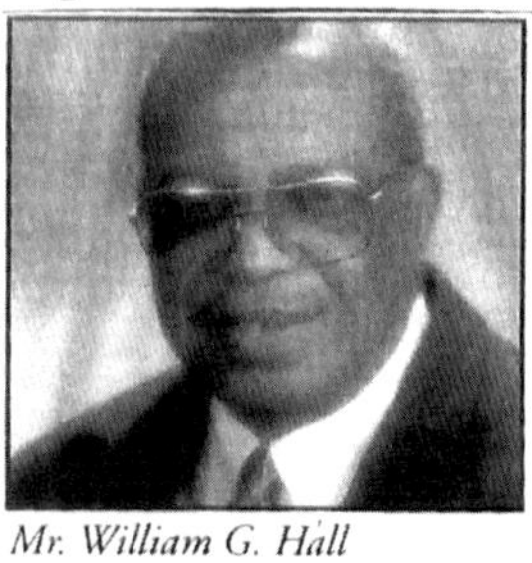

Mr. William G. Hall
Assistant Principal George Washington Carver

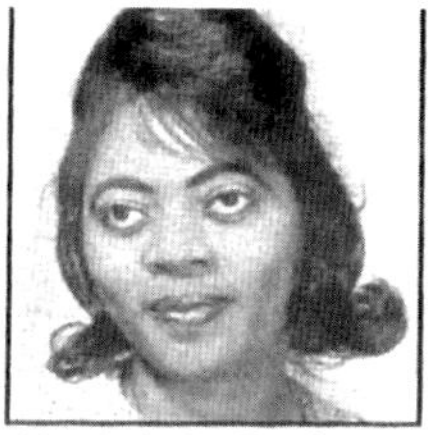
Mrs. Ruby L. Handcox

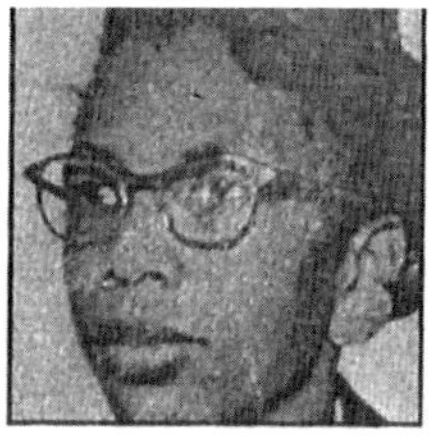
Mrs. Bettye J. Hatchett

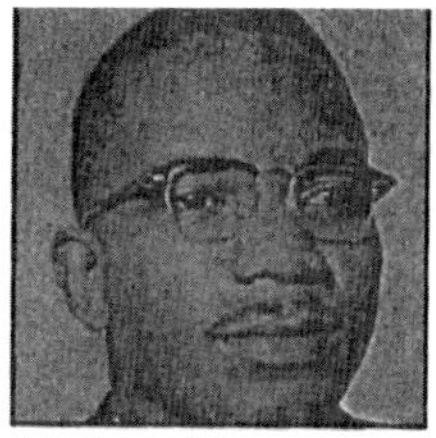
Mr. James Johnson

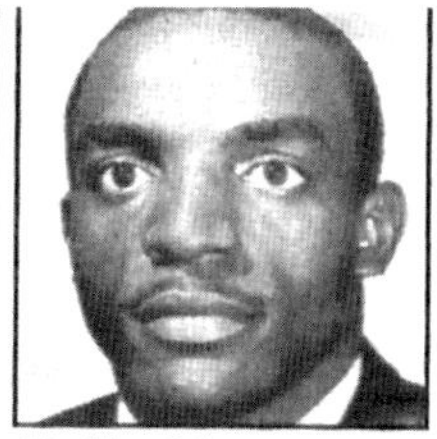
Mr. Troy Johnson

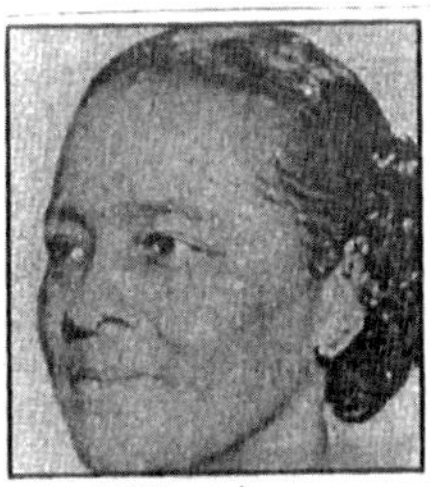
Mrs. Willia Johnson

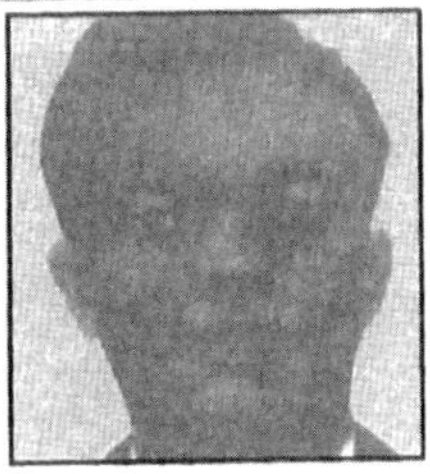
Mr. E. A. Kemp
Bryan Public School for Colored

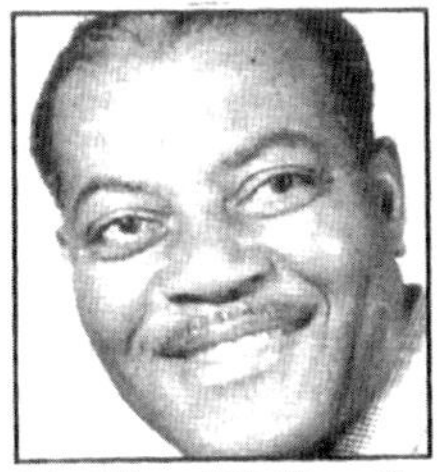
Mr. Edward H. Knox, Sr.
Washington Elementary

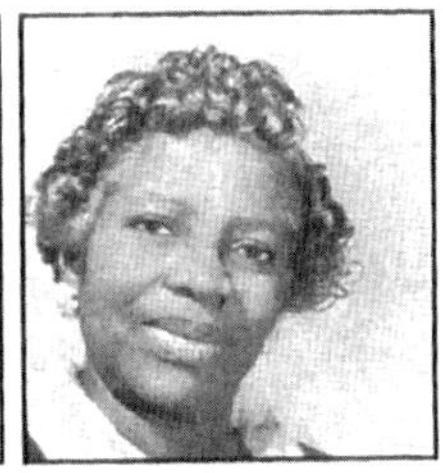
Mrs. Irene Lane

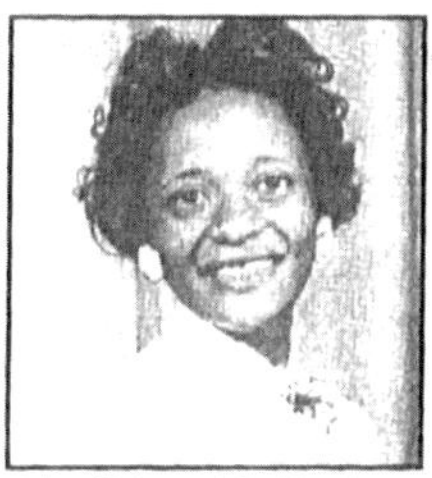
Mrs. Edessie McClendon

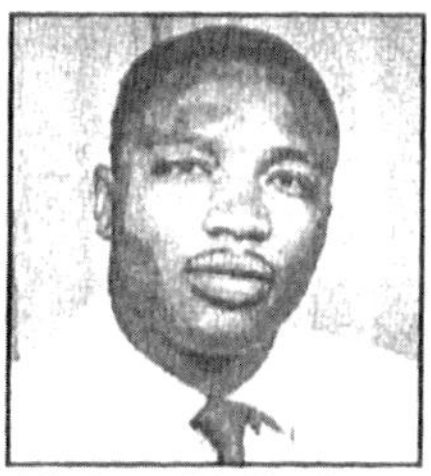
Mr. James McClendon

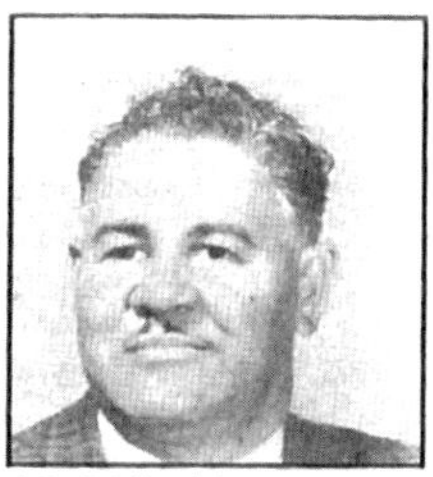
Mr. Willie Moore, Jr.

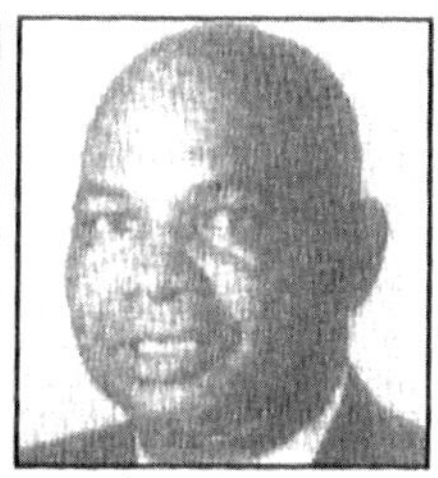
Mr. Ulysses S. Morgan
First Principal of R. C. Neal Junior High School

Above: Ruby L. Handcox, Bettye Hatchett and James Johnson all taught at E.A. Kemp Senior High. Mr. Troy Johnson (no relation) taught at E.A. Kemp Senior High, and Willia Johnson (no relation) taught at E.A. Kemp Junior-Senior High. Mr. E.A. Kemp was principal of Bryan Public School for Colored, and Mr. Knox was principal of Washington Elementary School. Irene Lane, who was a graduate of Bryan Public School for Colored, taught at E.A. Kemp Junior-Senior High, along with Edessie McClendon and Raymond Moore. Mr. Morgan was the first principal of R.C. Neal Junior High School. *Courtesy Dr. Adolph Johnson Jr.*

Opposite: The ten individuals pictured here are Mrs. Anderson and Mr. Guyden, who both started at E.A. Kemp Junior-Senior High School and continued at E.A. Kemp Senior High; Ms. Olivia Banks, who started at John M. Moore and continued at E.A. Kemp Senior High; Ms. Bailey and Ms. Cowan, who both started at E.A. Senior High; and Mr. Dunn, the school principal. Mr. Byrd was a teacher at John M. Moore before he became principal of George Washington Carver Elementary School. *Courtesy Dr. Adolph Johnson Jr.*

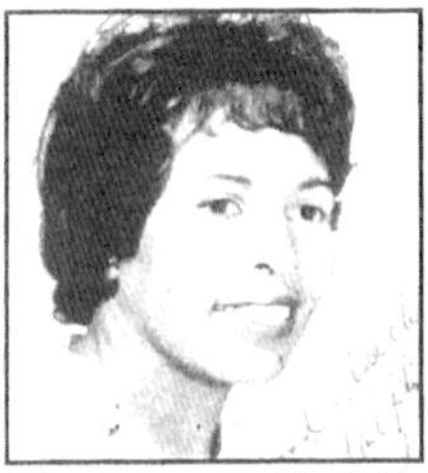
Mrs. Delores Stubberfield

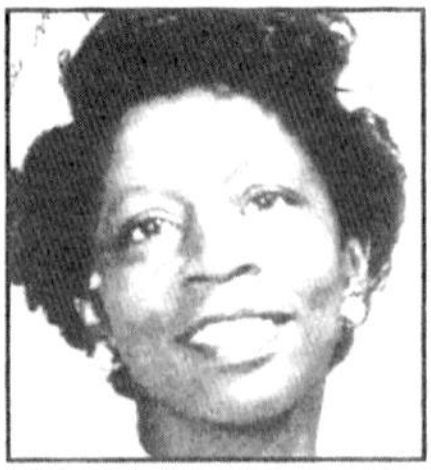
Mr. Edna Tarrow

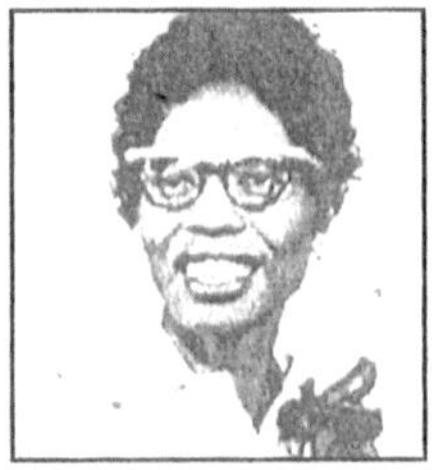
Mrs. Cora H. Tennant

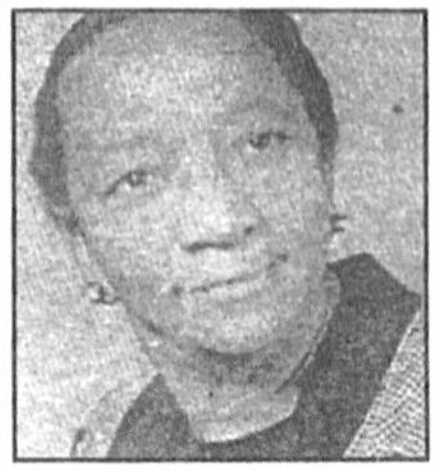
Mrs. Sadie Thomas

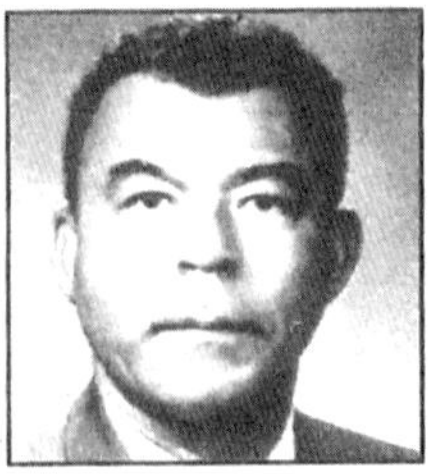
Mr. Lloyd Thomas

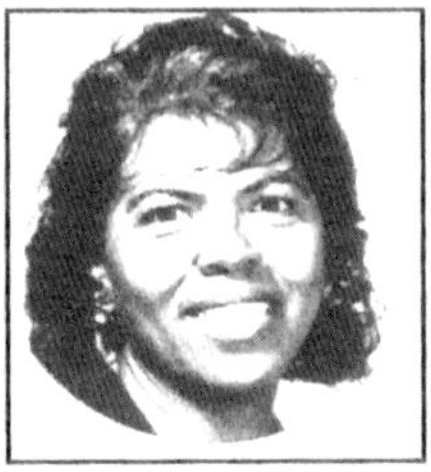
Mrs. Bernice Webster

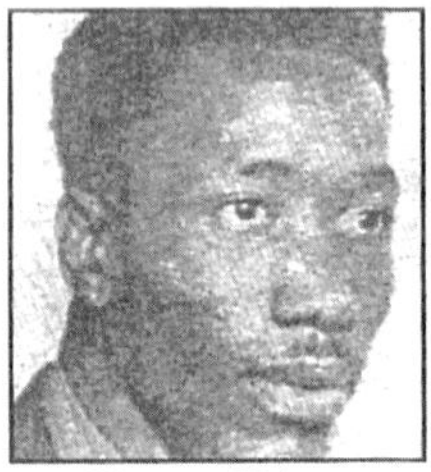
Mr. Waymon Webster

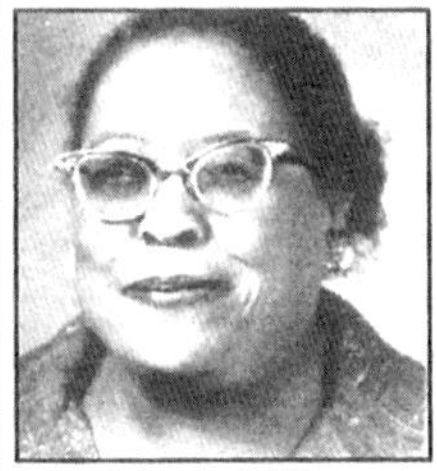
Mrs. Johnnie P. Wyatt

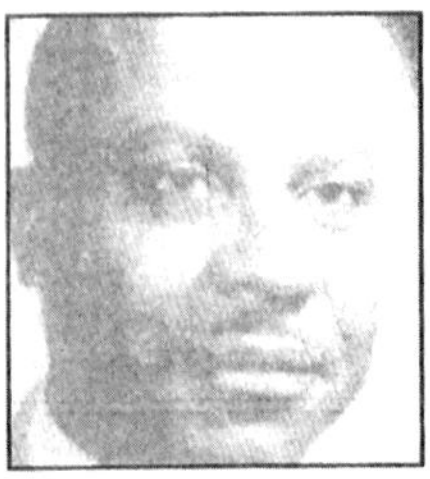
Mr. C. D. Yancy
George Washington Carver
E. A. Kemp Jr-Sr High

Delores Stubberfield (school librarian), Cora Tennant, Sadie Thomas, Lloyd Thomas, Bernice and Waymon Webster (husband and wife) and Johnnie P. Wyatt taught at E.A. Kemp Junior-Senior High and E.A. Kemp Senior High. Colquitt D. Yancy was the principal of George Washington Carver Elementary School before becoming E.A. Kemp Junior-Senior High's principal. *Courtesy Dr. Adolph Johnson Jr.*

CHAPTER THIRTEEN

DRY TOILETS, STREETLIGHTS, LAMPS AND UNPAVED STREETS

Salvation is being on the right road, not having reached a destination.
—Martin Luther King Jr.

For African Americans, life in Bryan was filled with separates, such as drinking fountains, theater seating, buses and trains. In addition, city services such as sewers, paved streets and streetlights were not equally available to African Americans as they were to whites. For example, Bryan built a sewage disposal plant in 1913 to accommodate the western part of the city, but a number of African American neighborhoods were not connected to the city sewer system until sometime in the mid-1940s. As a result, dry toilets (outhouses) dotted the landscape throughout both east and west side communities. But the city employed two African American citizens, Roger Harris and Jim Day, to clean and disinfect the facilities to prevent harmful bacteria from spreading. Another consequence of not being connected to the sewer system was using tin, galvanized tubs for personal hygiene and washing clothes. It was common to see women in African American neighborhoods with scrub boards in tin tubs and large black pots of boiling water as they did their laundry on the weekends.

According to the Brazos County Historical Time Line, streetlight construction began in 1919 in the residential areas of West Twenty-sixth and East Twenty-sixth Streets and near Fanin School in 1921. However, most African Americans lived on the north end of the city, and streetlights were not fully installed in that neighborhood until later. Not having streetlights did not deter boys from attending the circus on Highway 21 at Waco Street, but to be safe, they would go in groups. In the meantime, kerosene lamps were the source of light for students doing their homework and parents reading their Bibles. Parents and older neighbors who could not see well with lamps would ask young people to thread needles and read the Bible to them. Kerosene stoves, although not very effective, were used to cook with and heat by. Alternative sources for cooking and heating were coal and wood. As some families could not afford to buy coal or wood, Guy Barrow's pasture was an abundant source of wood for many families. C.L. Smith, Pinkey Parnell and others would cut wood by the cord and sell to families who could afford to buy.

In the absence of electricity, iceboxes were used to prevent perishable foods from spoiling and keep beverages cold. During this time, there were two ice deliverymen: Guy Barrow and Ira Mickens. One of my tasks was to empty the water pan from melted ice before it was full. On many occasions, the family would wake up in the morning to find water had overflowed all over the linoleum floor. Guy Barrow delivered ice in a horse-drawn wagon in twenty-five- to fifty-pound blocks. Ice melted rather quickly in the Texas heat, so when Ira Mickens began delivering ice in a truck, the ice lasted longer. Mr. Barrow stopped delivering ice soon after Mr. Mickens established a loyal customer base.

Another marked disparity in African American neighborhoods was unpaved streets. Although downtown Main Street was paved in 1915, children had to trudge muddy streets to school when it rained. Worse yet, the streets at night were so dark that students who lived on the east side on the far end of Waco Street had a difficult time trying to get to E.A. Kemp Junior-Senior High located on the west side. The same was true for students who lived on the west side at the far end of California Street (before Carver Elementary was built) who were trying to get to Washington Elementary School on the east side.

CHAPTER FOURTEEN

IRONIES, CONTRADICTIONS AND PARADOXES

There were two signs that read COLORED and WHITES ONLY that were prominently displayed at water fountains, bus stops and train stations and also at the library, theaters and restaurants. No matter about the signs and back doors, it was an absolute treat every Saturday to buy a chili hot dog served from the back door while whites of Bryan could use the front door. I often thought it ironic that during the Korean Conflict, African Americans who left Bryan for induction centers rode in the back part of the bus on their way to fight for a country that still relegated them to the margins of society.

The Thirteenth, Fourteenth and Fifteenth Amendments to the United States Constitution contain provisions pertaining to citizenship, representation and the right to vote. The Thirteenth Amendment (1865) forbids slavery in any state of the Union. The Fourteenth Amendment (1868) stipulates that all persons born in the United States are U.S. citizens and cannot be deprived of life, liberty or property without due process of law, nor can they be denied equal protection of the law. The Fifteenth Amendment (1870) forbids states to deny the right to vote to male citizens on account of race, color or previous condition of servitude. Yet, in 1866, the Texas state constitution still prohibited blacks from voting or holding public office. It did allow newly freed men the right to sue, be sued, contract and be contracted with. Although blacks were allowed to vote later and served in the state legislature, state law, at one time, required blacks to pay a poll tax in order to vote, which meant many African American citizens did not vote because they could not afford to pay the poll tax.

An article in the December 7, 1985 edition of the *Bryan Daily* reported that there were a total of thirty-one white schools and thirty-four "colored" schools in Brazos County. It was obvious that white and black schools were separate, but it was also clear they were not equal. On October 23, 1913, the *Eagle* reported the figures that the county superintendent, T.W. Parker, collected between September 1, 1912, and August 31, 1913:

Category	**White**	**Colored**	**Total**
Number of schools taught	34	37	71
Number of teachers employed	53	37	90
Number of pupils enrolled in school	1,782	1,763	3,545
Number of teachers holding permanent certificates	9	4	13
Number of teachers holding first-grade certificates	19	3	22
Number of teachers holding second-grade certificates	25	30	55
Number of school desks in use	1,262	57	1,319
Number of volumes in school libraries	1,086	10	1,096
Amount paid teachers	$20,299.90	$9,298.93	$29,598.83
Amount paid for repairing/ building schoolhouses	$3,834.69	$375.11	$4,209.80
Amount paid for school desks, school supplies, wood, etc.	$1,546.13	$69.10	$1,615.23
Estimated value of school property	$30,189.00	$4,042.00	$34,231.00
Average length of school term	7.5	5.75	6.63

A 1945–46 survey of Brazos County schools conducted by Superintendent Luther Pearson found that there were twenty-four common districts operating twenty-four white and Negro schools. Eleven of these districts did not have any schools that operated, causing the twenty-four schools to be distributed among thirteen districts. Of this number, ten were for whites and fourteen for colored children. There were eighteen white school buildings in the county with fifty classrooms and eighteen teachers. All buildings in the white schools met state requirements. The colored schools totaled twenty buildings with forty-nine classrooms in all and employed forty-three teachers. There were not any auditoriums in the colored buildings, and only four of them met state requirements.

All the buildings for whites had jacketed-wood circulating heaters and adequate light and ventilation. There was also plenty of blackboard space, and each child had a desk; however, in the colored schools, excepting two districts, all heaters were box heaters, lighting and ventilation was poor and, in the two largest schools, there were two pupils to each desk.

In 1954, Supreme Court judges in the landmark case *Brown v. Board of Education* declared that school segregation and the doctrine of separate but equal was unconstitutional. Bryan Public Schools did not fully integrate until 1971, when Stephen F. Austin and E.A. Kemp Senior High Schools merged into what is now Bryan (Vikings) Senior High School.

Further ironies, contradictions and paradoxes in the life and times of African Americans in Bryan, Texas, are reflected in the Handbook of Texas Online, under the section entitled "Education African Americans." The following information from this source is used (with permission) to illustrate the point of what happened in both the United States and Texas.

The education of African American children during the late period of slavery, after 1800, was sporadic and unreliable in Texas and in other southern states, and formal education was practically nonexistent for African Americans. Before the Civil War, most white people believed that educating African Americans would lead to discontent and rebellion. A few did support instruction and often volunteered their services. According to the 1850 census, African Americans represented 27.5 percent of the nation's population. Of those who lived in Texas, 397 (less than 1 percent) were free; 217 were believed to be literate; 20 were in school; and 58 were illiterate adults. There are no actual statistics available on the 58,151 enslaved African Americans, but available data indicates that a portion of the slave population had received basic education in reading and writing.

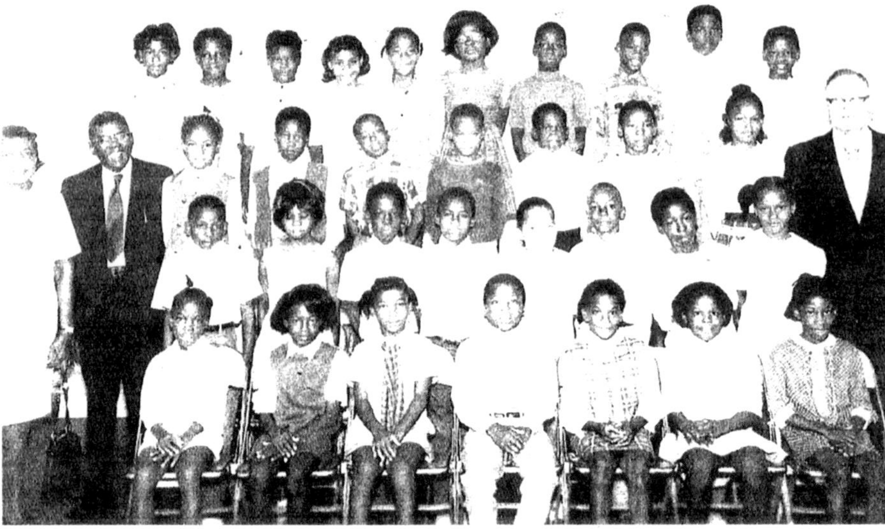

In 1970, African American students were bused to the all-white Fannin Elementary School. There were still segregated classrooms at this time. Bryan ISD was finally desegregated in 1971. *Courtesy* Up from Cotton *and Brazos Valley African American Museum.*

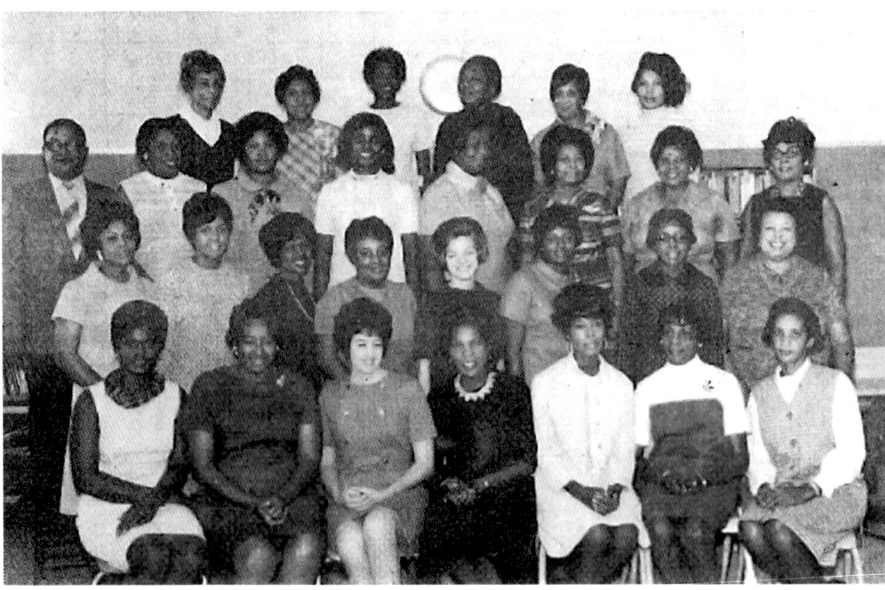

George Washington Carver Elementary School was built in 1949, and by the 1969–70 school year, all but two of the teachers were African American. The first African American teacher at the school, Otha Byrd (standing in the third row, to the left), served as its principal. *Courtesy* Up from Cotton *and Brazos Valley African American Museum.*

In 1865, the United States Congress instituted the Freedmen's Bureau, and its primary function was to supervise and coordinate a vast educational enterprise in Texas and sixteen other southern and border states, as well as the District of Columbia. The bureau supervised schools offering classes from the elementary level through college. These schools provided a formal curriculum of arithmetic, reading, writing, history and geography. In addition, a practical curriculum of civics, politics, home economics and vocational training was provided. Most teachers were supplied by the American Missionary Association, with the majority initially coming from the northern states. Soon thereafter, a few southern whites and educated African Americans were recruited to teach in these schools.

In January 1866, Texas began with ten-day and six-night schools for black children. There were 10 teachers with a total enrollment of 1,041 students, many of whom were adults. Six months later, on July 1, 1866, the Freedmen's Bureau in Texas had ninety schools (including day, night and Sabbath schools), 43 teachers and 4,590 students attending. John A. Alvord, the first and only inspector of schools and finances for the bureau, described Texas schools during this period as prosperous. He found that Texas's freedmen schools needed only minimal assistance from northern states and attributed this to what he perceived as the minimal impact of the Civil War upon the economic base of Texas. By the end of 1870, there were eighty-eight schools (both day and night) in Texas, 85 teachers (44 of whom were African American) and 4,478 students. In addition, there were twenty-seven Sabbath schools with 28 teachers (23 were black) and 1,350 students.

The advent of schools staffed by northern white missionaries was not acceptable to everyone in the white South. Some were alarmed by the mandatory acceptance of African Americans in state politics and vehemently opposed the Freedmen's Bureau. They even exhibited their resentment by burning schools and intimidating missionary teachers. But this attitude was not universal in Texas. The Texas Teachers' Convention of 1866, for example, passed a resolution urging training for the newly freed African Americans residing in Texas. Divergences of opinion and fluctuating attitudes were most distinctly revealed in legislative enactments from 1866 to 1876. The constitution of 1866 provided that the "income derived from the Public School Fund be employed exclusively for the education of white scholastic inhabitants" and that the "legislature may provide for the levying of a tax for educational purposes." The Reconstruction legislature of 1870 eliminated segregation and thereby gave Texas a single educational system, in which all children shared, but in 1873 and 1875, the state legislature repealed most of the laws of the Reconstruction period.

In 1871, Texas organized a public school system. The succeeding system, formed under the constitution of 1876, reestablished the segregation of races but made impartial provisions for each. Between 1873 and 1893, blacks met at state conventions and expressed their opinions to delineate their needs and to shape educational policies. The most significant were the Waco and Brenham conventions, as well as the Colored Teachers Association's first meeting in Austin in 1884. The Texas Board of Education conducted its first survey of black schools in 1921. At that time, 6,369 pupils were enrolled. By 1925, there were 150 institutions in Texas offering one or more years of high school work for African Americans. This included 14 city high schools, 6 or more county high schools and high school departments in every junior and senior college. In the 1920s to 1930s, the average length of the school term for black children was only about four days shorter than that for white children. However, the State of Texas spent an average of $3.39, about one-third less for the education of African American students than for white students. During the same period, black teachers were paid significantly less than white teachers ($91.60 a month, compared with $121.03). In 1940, there were 222,715 black pupils in 116 accredited Texas high schools, 12 of which were rated by the Southern Association of Colleges and Secondary Schools. Approximately half of the 6,439 teachers had degrees.

CHAPTER FIFTEEN

TEACHERS, PARENTS AND CHURCHES

What I Have Learned

You must step out of the field before you can see the mud on your feet.
—Chinese proverb

Growing up, there were three strong institutions in the African American community: schools, parents and the church. They operated in tandem, and I still believe they were responsible for what students achieved in the years that Bryan was segregated and even after. One of the things I shared at the start of this book was my intention to have a written document about African Americans from Bryan ready for the reunion of 2010. I also stated that events and people not included in the first project would be mentioned in any subsequent project. Preparing this project, as in the first one, helped me to remember events and individuals who provided unforgettable guidance and support at critical stages of life. It also helped me to better understand the Chinese saying included above.

Additionally, the work I have done researching and preparing this book has allowed me to reflect seriously about why former students of the Bryan Public School for Colored, E.A. Kemp Junior-Senior High and E.A. Kemp Senior High from the years 1948 to 1950 come back every two (starting in 2012 for Bryan Colored) and five years for reunions. Perhaps two of the reasons why students come for reunions are in the purpose section of the alumni bylaws: to retain the identity of E.A. Kemp High and promote the highest standards of socialization. They may also come back because they realize that these schools and those employed at them in the years Bryan was segregated helped to shape who blacks of Bryan have become. But also, we come back to say thanks for starting us on our way and to honor all three schools because they, we learned later, were preparing us for a world we could scarcely imagine. The importance of each one of these institutions, schools, teachers, parents and churches is demonstrated at each reunion. The reunion starts with a church service, where teachers and parents are recognized, and it ends with a church service. Although our teachers worked under difficult conditions and in dismal circumstances, they were able to instill hope and lift spirits of students who had so little. Teachers not only taught English, history, math and science, but they also taught inspiration and endurance and would not allow students to quit, as reflected in the following poem by Hazel Felleman:

When things go wrong, as they sometimes will,
When the road we are trudging seems up hill,
When the funds are low and the debts are high,
And we want to smile, but have to sigh,
When care is pressing you down a bit,
Rest if you must-but don't quit.

At E.A. Kemp, teachers treated students with respect and dignity; we were not marginalized. It was our preparation ground for learning how to live with others; the golden rule and limits were things self-imposed. E.A. Kemp was where students learned they had promises to keep and miles to go before they could sleep. The teachers helped students understand the meaning of the words James Renick used in his inauguration speech when he was made chancellor of North Carolina Agricultural State University: "Heights of great men and women were not reached in sudden flight, but they, while others slept, toiled through the night."

It is amazing today that some young people of privilege and wealth experience epidemic rates of depression and anxiety. They lack a sense of authentic self; in other words, they possess wealth but not mental health—a stark contrast to the African American boys and girls who grew up in Bryan and were, for the most part, very confident and self-assured. But then there's the question of why. Perhaps it was the special hymns—"Blessed Assurance Jesus Is Mine," "Jesus Keeps Me Near the Cross" or "Amazing Grace"—or the song "I Come to the Garden Alone Where the Dew Is Still on the Roses" that students sang at weekly school assemblies.

Hymns that were heard and sung at school and home helped to create a vital balance.

Other reasons why individuals come back to reunions are triggered by memories of Mass, religious education and sacraments at Immaculate Conception, Sunday church school and vacation Bible school, as well as experiences at Allen Chapel, Lee Chapel, Peaceful Rest and Shiloh located on the east side. The same is true for individuals on the west side who participated in Sunday church school and vacation Bible school at Pleasant Grove, Galilee and New Chapel. After all, the churches, parents and teachers were the foundational blocks upon which character was built and life compasses set. The church experiences and parents taught us to "Lean On the Ever Lasting Arm…Truth Crushed to Earth Shall Rise Again, Truth Forever on the Scaffold, Wrong forever on the Throne, Yet that Scaffold sways the future, and behind the dim unknown Stand God within the shadow, Keeping watch above his own." What parents, especially mothers, taught as part of the trilogy is epitomized in the modified words of Langston Hughes's poem "Mother to Son":

Life won't be a crystal stair
It will have tacks in it
And splinters—boards torn up, floors
That are bare. But all the time you must keep
Climbing on—reaching landings and turning
Corners. And sometimes going in the dark, where
There ain't no light.

This project, as do reunions, afforded an opportunity to return to what are often referred to as the "good old days"—a chance to travel back in time and space and recall activities, friends and situations that were happy as well as sad. Some of the happy times were attending homecoming parades, football games, post-game socials, gatherings at Knox's Place, a first date with a special boy or girl, prom night and graduation. This experience provided an opportunity for me to safely review the past and the distance traveled since leaving Kemp High. It also reminded me of how far we have yet to go.

Finally, students come back to E.A. Kemp reunions because attendance at Kemp High is another one of the commonly shared experiences. No matter where you lived in Bryan, east side or west or any of the surrounding areas, Kemp was the only high school for African Americans until after 1971.

CHAPTER SIXTEEN

POPULATION RECORDS FOR BRAZOS COUNTY AND BRYAN, TEXAS, 1900–2010

According to Brundige, African Americans played a vital part in the initial and continued economic development of Brazos County, but their influence was limited because of segregation. In 1890, the number of African Americans reached 8,845—the first and only time in its history that Brazos County experienced a black majority. Based on census information taken from the Handbook of Texas Online, the total populations of Brazos County and Bryan, Texas, continued to grow. But only a few documents reviewed for this project contained a breakdown of the African American population. The information below is from the Handbook of Texas Online.

Year	Report Name	Population
1900	Brazos County Census reports Brazos County population	18,859
1900	Bryan Census reports Bryan's population	3,589
1910	Brazos County Census reports Brazos County population	18,919
1910	Bryan Census reports Bryan's population	4,132
1920	Brazos County Census reports Brazos County population	21,975
1920	Bryan Census reports population	6,307
1930	Brazos County Census reports Brazos County population	21,835*

1930	Bryan Census reports Bryan's population	7,814
1940	Brazos County Census reports Brazos County population	26,799
1940	Bryan Census reports Bryan's population	11,842
1950	Brazos County Census reports Brazos County population	38,390
1950	Bryan Census reports Bryan's population	18,102
1960	Brazos County Census reports Brazos County population	44,895
1960	Bryan Census reports Bryan's population	27,542
1970	Brazos Census reports Brazos County population	57,978
1970	Bryan Census reports Bryan's population	33,719
1980	Brazos County Census reports Brazos County population	93,588
1980	Bryan Census reports Bryan's population	44,337
1990	Brazos County Census reports Brazos County population	121,862
1990	Bryan Census reports Bryan's population	55,002
2000	Brazos County Census reports Brazos County population	152,415
2000	Bryan Census reports Bryan's population	65,660
2010	Brazos County Census reports Brazos County population	194,851
2010	Bryan Census reports Bryan's population	76,201

*Slight loss in county population, no explication given

The racial makeup of the 2000 population in Bryan, Texas, was 64.65 percent (65 percent) white, 17.7 percent (18 percent) African American and 22.47 percent Mexican American. The 2000 U.S. Census of Bryan reports the total population for that year was 65,660. The 2010 U.S. census for Bryan reports a total population of 76,201, an increase of 16.1 percent. In 2010, the racial makeup of the population in Bryan was 64.22 percent white, 18 percent African American and 36.24 percent Hispanic-Latino. Unlike the 2000 census, the 2010 census did not have a category for Mexican Americans. Instead, the 2010 census incorporated Mexican American into the Hispanic-Latino grouping, hence the large increase in that population's percentage.

CHAPTER SEVENTEEN

SURPRISE FINDINGS

Here is additional information about events and people discovered while doing research that may be of interest. The dates and events from 1865 to 1970 recorded below were taken from the Brazos County Historical Time Line. Later information about events, people and places after 1971 was confirmed or verified through interviews and site visits.

1865	December	Bryan: W.W. Davis opens a freedmen's school in Bryan
1867	February	Brazos County: Stephen Curtis, an African American, is elected as delegate to the State Constitution Convention
1870	September	Bryan: Shiloh Baptist Church purchases land
	December	Bryan: Conference of African American Methodist Episcopal Church (AME) meets
1874	March	Bryan: City sells the "Freedmen Burying Ground" to local church
1875	February	Bryan: Stearne Chapel African American Church is given land
1877	December	Bryan: Conference of AME Church meets

1878	September	Brazos County: An African American temperance organization is founded
	November	Brazos County: Elias Mayes, an African American, is elected to the Texas Legislature*
1879	February	Bryan: Cornerstone for Allen Chapel is laid
	August	Bryan: Rev. S.W. Marston from St. Louis holds institute for "colored ministers"
1880	October	Bryan: Bryan public school for colored students has twenty students**
1882	December	Bryan: Conference of AME Church meets
1883	September	Bryan: Blacks sue for right to ride in first-class railroad coaches
1888	November	Brazos County: Several African Americans are elected to offices; Elias Mayes (Mays in some records) is again elected to Texas Legislature; H.M. Maddox and D.B. Ballard are elected county commissioners; Powell Harvey is elected constable
1890	June	Brazos County: A.H. Colwell is replaced as a census taker by a white man
1894	August	Bryan: Principal A.H. Colwell is nominated by the Republican Party to be superintendent of education; colored branch of the Grand United Order of Old Fellows meets
1896	December	Bryan: Conference of AME Church meets at Allen Chapel
1898		Bryan: Shiloh Baptist Church purchases land
1899		Bryan: Colored Masonic Grand Lodge meets
	June	Bryan: Conference of AME Church meets
1900		Bryan: African American Deputy Sheriff Levi Neal is killed in the line of duty.
	February	Bryan: Sewage disposal plant is completed
1901		Bryan: Paul Landry becomes principal of Bryan Public School for Colored

1903	January	Bryan: Colored citizens establish a burial organization
	August	Bryan: An anti-Prohibition club for blacks is organized
1904	July	Bryan: Colored branch of the Ancient Order of Pilgrims meets
1905	June	Brazos County: Pleasant Grove Baptist Church holds opening services for new building
	October	Bryan: Farmers Improvement Society of Texas (colored) meets
1906	October	Bryan: Cornerstone laid for new Lee Chapel building
1908	September	Bryan: Local African American farmers organize a farmers' union
1912		Bryan: Dr. S.W. Hooks opens a drugstore
1913	January	Bryan: The "colored" YMCA is organized*
1918		Bryan: Blacks form a Red Cross Auxiliary
	May	Bryan: Negro Business League is formed
	October	Bryan: Negro Council of Defense is formed
1919	February	Brazos County: Colored Ministers Association meets at Shiloh Baptist Church
	April	Bryan: Local NAACP chapter is organized
1920	March	Brazos County: Cornerstone for the second Allen Chapel building is laid
	July	Bryan: Colored Woodmen of the World meets
1922	June	Bryan: Grandview Colored Cemetery opens
1923	November	Brazos County: A Good Cheer organization is formed to help area blacks in need
1929	June	Bryan: Dr. William A. Hammond Sr. is elected president of the Texas African American Medical Association
	June	Bryan: Professor E.A. Kemp dies
1931	September	Bryan: E.A. Kemp Junior-Senior High opens*

1938	January	Brazos County: Negro Worker's Club is organized
	February	Brazos County: African Americans interested in scouting meet
1942	April	Bryan: Groundbreaking for Negro Catholic Church (Immaculate Conception)
1959		Bryan: Sadie E. Thomas Memorial Park is dedicated

*Cited in text earlier
**Not to be confused with Bryan Public School for Colored, founded in 1885

According to an article entitled "The Black Experience in Brazos County" that was published in the February 8, 1986 edition of the *Bryan-College Station Eagle*, two black newspapers, the *Republican* and *Torchlight*, were established in 1895 and 1912. The *Republican* was founded in 1895 by Reverend R.M. Holmes, who had previously published the *Watchword*. The *Torchlight* was founded in 1912.

CHAPTER EIGHTEEN
AFRICAN AMERICANS STILL RISING

SMALL BUSINESSES AND OTHER VENTURES

Some, not all, African Americans who were not mentioned in previous chapters but who continued to demonstrate self-reliance by establishing small businesses, gaining employment and pursuing higher education and the private sector are indicated below.

Johnny Ellis, class of 1954, started Trucking and Vending Machine, Inc.

Ray McDade, M.C. Scott and Walter Jr. owned trucking companies.

Paul Madison, class of 1965, was owner of Metals and Business Consultants.

Elvin Walker, class of 1963, opened Presto Car Wash in 1976, KWIK-KAR Car Wash in 1984 and another car wash in 1999. Elvin also became the first African American detective sergeant on the Bryan Police Force.

Jesse Marvin Walker established a bail bondsman office in 1987 and is also the owner of Walker and Walker Custom Printing.

Irma Rooks Kearney experimented with a "Rent-A-Nanny" service in the 1980s.

Melvin Hanks owned Family Realtors and Curry Plumbing Inc., two going business concerns in Bryan.

Willie Idlebird owned Bird's Appliance Services.

Ples Turner was a builder and contractor.

Raymond Johnson owned several service stations named Green and Sons.

Thomas L. Moore owns an appliance and repair service.
Bessie Gibbs Mason owned a Christian bookstore.
Ann E. King owns an African American book and specialty store.
Amy Bradley Galloway owned a domestic cleaning service.

The following are names and businesses that have been included in this book that were not in the previous book:

Leon Ellis, owner of In Style Barbershop
Wanda Goo, owner of Creative Hair Design
Rhonda Seyfus, owner of U-Nik Kuts by Rhonda
Lurls, Beauty and Barber
Vivian Vaults Rawls, owner of Rawls and Associate
A.W. Johnson Trucking, Inc.
William B. Johnson Sr.'s Johnson's Homebody Properties
James' Studio 59
Denise Nichols, owner of VIP Music and Book Store
Thomas and Jenita Rayford Transports
Kenneth Robinson, owner of Daniel and Son Funeral Home
Robert Carter, owner of Enterprise Advisory Services

PUBLIC SCHOOLS, GOVERNMENT, HIGHER EDUCATION, PRIVATE SECTOR, CORPORATE

Mrs. Linda Smith Asberry is principal of Neal Elementary School in Bryan.

Dr. Sid Garner was principal of Robert Driscoll Middle School in Corpus Christi.

George Vaults began his professional education career as a teacher at George Washington Carver Elementary School in Bryan. He subsequently served as an elementary and junior high school principal and was also high school principal of B.C. Moore Senior High School. After serving as high school principal, he became deputy superintendent in the North Forest Independent School District. His final public school administration post was as superintendent of the Calvert ISD, during which time he was voted superintendent of the year for region four in 1994. Mr. Vaults was part of Texas Southern University's faculty and served at the Texas Education Agency.

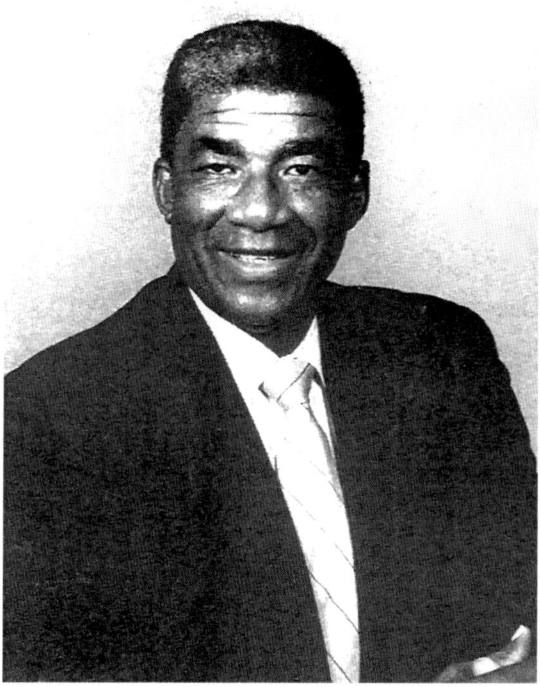

Mr. George Vaults, a 1954 E.A. Kemp graduate, has worked as a teacher in Bryan's public school system and was also superintendent of the Calvert ISD. He was voted superintendent of the year for region four in 1994. *Courtesy George Vaults.*

Bobby Joe Perry, the head basketball coach at E.A. Kemp, led the team to victory in the district championship in 1968–69. He also led Bryan High Vikings to four district championships and two bi-district championships and was named coach of the year in 1972–73.

Blanche Barrow and Johnny Robertson taught in American Indian schools on Arizona reservations.

Beverley Sheppard Lawson is the department chair of the career and technical education department in the Fort Bend ISD.

Mildred Ray Davis served as assistant superintendent of the Grand Prairie ISD.

Queen E. Vaults Shaw was director of staff development in the North Forest ISD.

Jo Ann Stephney Jordan served as a public school principal in a Northern California Independent School District.

Barbara Jean Rucker Broussard was a computer specialist in the Houston ISD.

Clovis D. Pruitt worked for Job Corps in San Antonio, Texas.

U.S. postal employees (since the first African Americans) include LaRue Johnson, Ples Turner, Odis Walton Sr., Savannah Williams, Charles Walton, Maurice Green Jr., Cecil Davis Crenshaw and Mattie Robinson Carter.

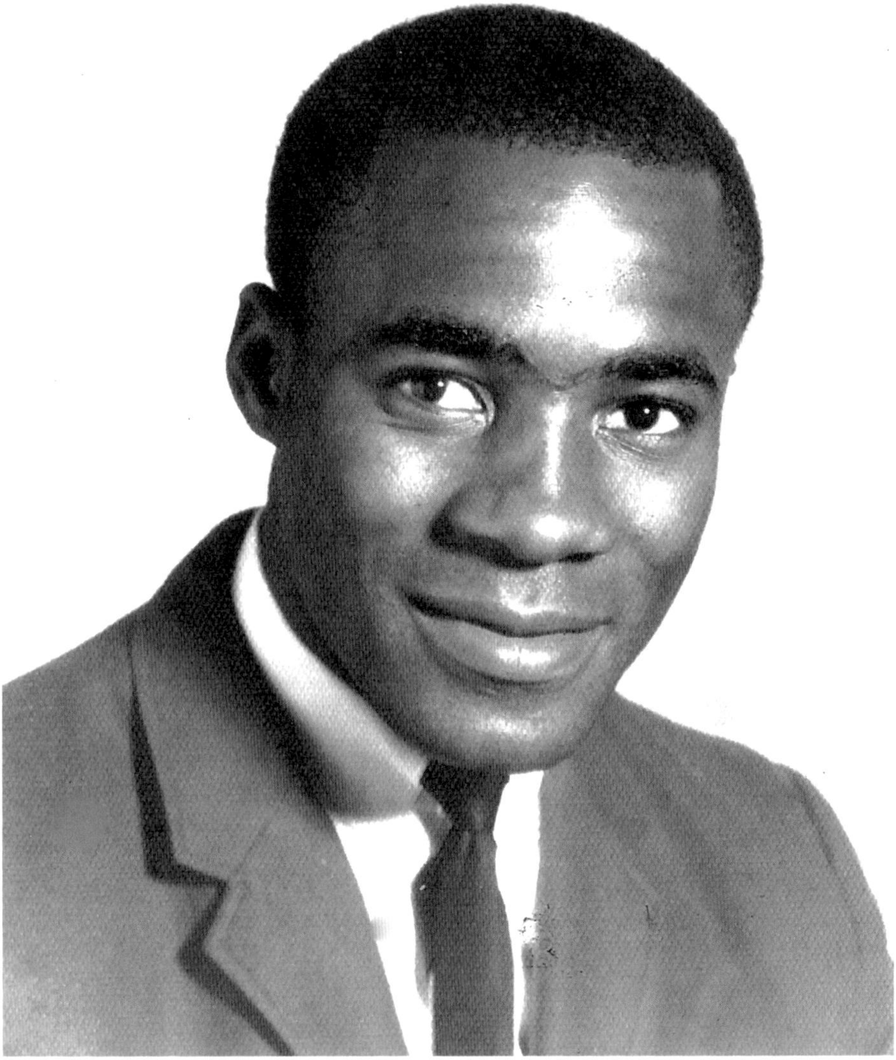

Mr. Bobby Joe Perry graduated from E.A. Kemp and returned after college graduation to coach at his alma mater. He became the head basketball coach and led the varsity team to the 1968–69 District 10 AAA North Zone Championship. Mr. Perry was also head basketball coach of the Bryan High Vikings, an integrated school. *Courtesy Mr. Perry and Brazos Valley African American Museum.*

Ernest Moore was in the Federal Civil Service in San Antonio and taught in the government vocational training school.

Peter Calhoun and Joe Willie Toliver are retired law enforcement officers for the cities of Los Angeles and Seattle, respectively.

Dr. Wendell Davis Jr. was an assistant professor at Prairie View A&M University and also the program director for the Division of Accreditation and Technical Assistance at the Texas Education Agency (TEA). He also served in the TEA's special investigations department and worked for the U.S. Department of Education.

Dr. Halcyon Sadberry Watkins was an assistant professor and assistant dean at Prairie View A&M University and was also an assistant professor at Texas Southern University.

Dr. J. (Joe) Willard Toliver was an instructor at Prairie View A&M University, a professor at the University of Houston, associate dean and professor at Florida A&M University and the associate dean at Florida State University's School of Engineering.

Leroy Sterling was an assistant professor at Alabama A&M University and Jarvis Christian College.

Walter Hollins is an assistant professor at Houston Community College.

Dr. Adolph Johnson Jr. served as academic dean at Cerritos Community College in California.

Barbara Williams Dixon was an instructor at Prairie View A&M University.

Gladys Green Smith served as associate dean of the Los Angeles Trade-Technical College.

Melvin Eugene Turner served as a priest at St. Phillips Episcopal Church.

Dr. Catherine Martin was on the faculty at both Prairie View A&M University and Tulane University.

Dr. Jerry Guyden is a professor at City College of New York.

Frank Perry was a member of the faculty at Florida A&M, Alcorn University (Mississippi), Texas Southern University, Jarvis Christian College, Fayetteville University (North Carolina), Stillman College (Alabama) and Livingstone College (North Carolina). He also studied at the prestigious Juilliard School of Music in New York.

James Sterling was assistant professor at Southern University in New Orleans and was hailed the highest-ranking African American in the marketing division at Dow Chemicals. He was also a scientist for the Federal Food and Drug Administration.

Dr. Darlene Sheppard Abram served as dean of the College of Education at Langston University in Oklahoma.

Dr. Weldon Walton was a member of the biology department, the chair of the science department and vice-president for academic affairs at Paul Quinn College.

O.D. Baker was an instructor at Houston Theological Seminary.

Willie Pruitt Jr. and Cecil Webster were members of the faculty at West Point Military Academy.

Dr. Wauline Pierce Gamble taught elementary school in the Caldwell ISD and was also a professor of education at Paul Quinn College.

Ethel Gibbs Batten was vice-president of human resources for Lucent Technologies in Warren, New Jersey. She was also vice-president of the Equal Opportunity and Human Resources Compliance Office for America, Canada and Latin America. In addition, Ethel was the vice-president of human resources at Global Diversity Operations for over 140 countries. She trained at the Aspen Institute, Cornell University, the University of Michigan and Yale University.

Juanita Gibbs Johnson served on the Federal Reserve Board.

Margaret Gibbs Brooks was an assistant vice-president for Urban Banking in Dallas.

Howard Gibbs is a labor relations specialist for the U.S. Postal Service in Oakland, California.

Leroy Gibbs worked as a manager for General Motors in Los Angeles.

James O. Gibbs was the senior quality control supervisor for General Motors in Los Angles.

Margaret R. Rucker Finely was a supervisor with Texaco Oil Company in Houston.

John Latson is a supervisor at the All Seasons Door and Window Company.

Leon Davis was a business manager for Hod Carriers Local 166 in Oakland, California.

Jimmy Leon Tillery was in the executive management tier for a telephone company in California.

Erma Faye Heads Jefferson was valedictorian for the class of 1958 and was one of the first African American female students to attend Texas A&M University. She was one of the co-founders and a member of the Black Coalition of Black Democrats and Outstanding Woman of Brazos County in 1983. She was an on-site financial monitor for the Texas Department of Housing and Community Affairs.

Beverly Nutall served on the board of directors of the American Association of Office Nurses, was the advisory editor of *License Professional*

Nurse Magazine and was appointed by Governor Rick Perry to the State Board of Nurse Examiners.

African American students who pursued professional careers had great role models. For example, the following husbands and wives had between sixty and seventy-five combined years teaching and working in administration: W.A. and Edna Tarrow, Willie and Mel Pruitt, Robert and Willie Neal, Lorenzo C. and Doris Scurry and John T. and Irene Lane, to name a few. Other public school teachers and administrators who have continued the long line of dedicated years of service from the 1920s to 1971 are arranged below by name and year of graduation from high school.

Classes of the 1920s

Olivia M. Banks
Douglas Littleton
Pearline Westbrook-Robinson
Johnnie L. Pillows Wyatt

Class of 1931

Lawrence King
Eddie Talley-Hall

Class of 1934

Blanche Barrow
Richard Dix

Class of 1935

Thay Myrtle Adams
Lawrence Wallace

Class of 1936

Louise Green

Class of 1937

Lorraine Johnson
Channie Dix Jordan
Ural Ocheltee
Berthenia Ellis Wallace
Jessie M. Hunter Walton

Class of 1938

Ikie M. Cashaw-Cooper
Doris Stearne

Class of 1939

Zack Grays

Class of 1942

Esterlene Moore-Randolph
Ruth Neal
Beatrice Potts

Class of 1944

Ethel Ford-Shipmon
Inez Johnson-Grays
Thelma Moore-Buchanan
Madelyn Westbrook-Burley

Class of 1945

Irene Shields Mitchell
Earnestine Petty

Class of 1946

Ella Mae Neal-Donovan
Prudence Sheppard-Byrd
Ulysses Wallace

Class of 1948

Rosie Rice Greer

Class of 1949

Jessie L. Cashaw
Ethel Gilmore
Pearlie Prunella Petty
Martha Potts Scott
Lorraine Sterling

Class of 1950

Hiawatha Dix-Godine
Dr. Wauline Pierce Gamble
Imogene Petty
Johnnie Petty

Class of 1951

Jessie Davenport-Devrow
Davis Edwards
Drusilla Gilmore
Ethel Lillian Jones
Estella Woods

Class of 1952

Dorelia Powell
Gladys Sanders

Class of 1953

Martha Miller Allen
Rosa Rouse Davis
Cleo Gilmore
Mazie Nell Smith Mark
Mary F. Bradley-Wells

Class of 1954

Doris Green Coleman
Doris Dix
Arthur Dunn
Frankie Morris
Blossie T. Phillips
Katha Robertson
George Vaults

Class of 1955

Iona Potts Griggs
Ann E. King
John Jerome Knox
Doris Ford Taylor
John L. Williams

Class of 1956

James T. Knox*
Billy Ray S.

Class of 1957

Louise Dix
Milton Green
David Littleton
Dearest Mack-Ray
Faye Patterson Sabbs

Class of 1958

O.D. Baker
Iney Cunningham
Etta Duren Jones
Vivian Faye Littleton
Raymond Moore
Lonnie Mulkey
Ona McMillian Sims
Janice Thurman

Class of 1959

Andrew Byrd Jr.
Bobbie Jean Idlebird
Gloria Knox
Clarence Mack
Christine Rice-Williams

Class of 1960

James H. Alberson
William G. Hall
Bobby Joe Perry
Betty Suseberry Hanks
Jesse M. Walker
Billie J. White-Lamb

Class of 1961

Johnnie M. Moten
Hayward Peterson
Shirley Steverson-Eaton

Class of 1962

Woodrow Jackson
Ruby Johnson Abel
Ellen Johnson
Wanda Peterson Green
Effie Perry
Eddied Mae Phillips

Class of 1963

Ruby J. Butler
Ivy Idlebird
Wanda Peterson-Green
Johnny Robertson

Class of 1964

Merilyn Evans
Willie Faye Paul-Walton
Albert Griffin

Class of 1965

Myrtle Allen-Rowe
Maxine Idlebird
Oletha Johnson-Bell
Ernestine Johnson-Tyler
Ernestine Suseberry-Hanks

Class of 1966

Pearl Collins Cavitts
Jo Ann Jordan
Lawson
Gloria Page
Robert Person
Calvin Phillips++
Mildred Ray-Davis
Wilma Robinson-Stewart
Beverly Sheppard
Linda Smith-Asberry
Karen Walton

Class of 1967

Shaw
Doris Thompson-Foreman
Queen E. Vaults

Class of 1968

Sharon Shipman-Kirwood

Class of 1969	Class of 1970	Class of 1971
Gwendolyn Davis	Clovis Pruitt	Agnes Goins-Gray
Claudette Scurry		Lorenzo Scurry
Patricia Toliver-Thornton		Vivian Vaults Rawls

*Became a registered pharmacist in Illinois later
++ Transferred senior year from E.A. Kemp to Stephen F. Austin

CHAPTER NINETEEN
BRYAN IN TRANSITION

In its early history, Bryan was largely a cotton commodity town, full of gins, compresses, yards, warehouses and rail connections to cotton farmers in the Brazos River Bottom. That it was a town with a large cotton- and agricultural-based economy had a lot to do with location. Centrally located in Texas, Bryan was ideally suited for cotton farmers in the Brazos Bottom, as its rail connectivity allowed farmers to ship their products throughout Brazos Valley and beyond. The founding of the Agricultural and Mechanical College in College Station also contributed to Bryan's development and scientific understanding of agriculture, mechanics and business acumen of a growing community.

Bryan today is a much different city than it was in 1885 and even in 1971. As stated in the earlier chapters, segregation was the dominant social issue during this period, especially in public schools. Segregation not only impacted public school education, but it also pervaded many aspects of African American life. Hence, the primary purpose of this chapter is to show how the city has changed (and is changing still) as it progressed, moving in a direction that is inclusive and decidedly different from earlier decades.

Perhaps seeds of change were planted in 1968 when an African American was elected to the city council. In 1968, Harmon "Son" Bell was the first African American to be elected to the Bryan City Council. He won the election, filling a vacancy from an unexpired term, but was reelected in 1969 in his own right and served as mayor pro tem.

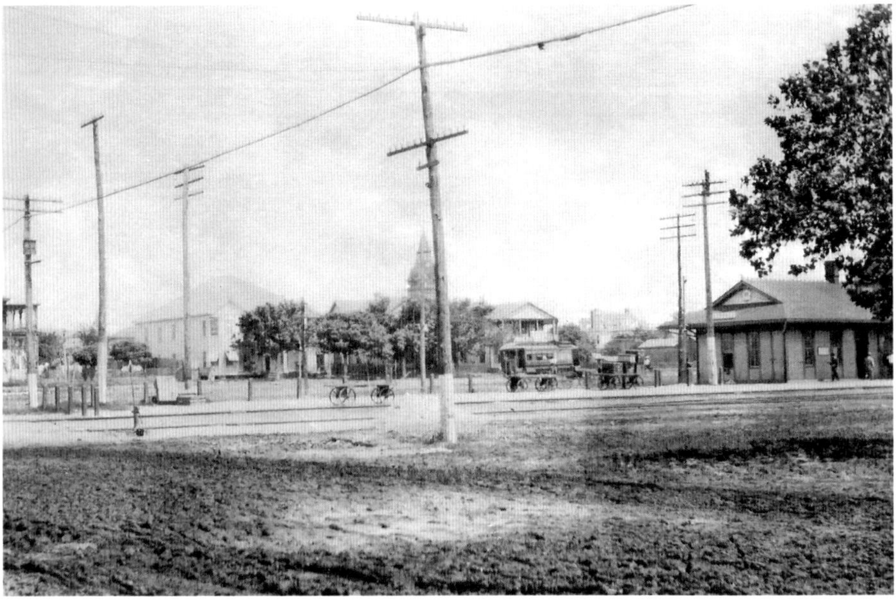

Pictured here are early train tracks and a railroad station that carried the cotton from the rich cotton fields in the Brazos Bottom throughout the Brazos Valley. *Courtesy Carnegie History Center.*

There are many signs that indicate the city has made strides toward removing some of the barriers that previously thwarted the aspirations of its African American citizens—barriers such as accommodations, education, employment, government and healthcare. There is also a general shift in attitude, as demonstrated by the signs one sees upon entering the city that read "Bryan: A Service Community," "A Good Place to Live" and the slogan "The Good Life Texas Style." In fact, Bryan now brags that it is a city of diversity. There are no longer restrictions where one can eat, sleep, live, purchase property and attend public affairs, events and functions. The LaSalle Hotel, for example, once denied accommodations for African Americans, but today, it is one among many of the choice hotels for those who attend E.A. Kemp alumni reunions. Many minorities are employed at institutions that once denied their admission. The City of Bryan hired an African American chief of police in 2007. Such employment would have been unthinkable years ago in Bryan. Other advancements made over the years include Texas A&M University appointing its first female president, which had an impact on Bryan's relationship and development. Bryan ISD has had at least one female superintendent of schools and has recently hired the first African American principal for the Bryan Senior High School. Bryan ISD has also had an African American male sit on its school board and currently has one African American female serving on the board of trustees. These are all changes in the right direction.

Bryan is a city with a master plan, encouraging the participation of all of its citizens in helping it become a city of pride and vitality. Further evidence of change can be observed through the city sponsoring events and festivals, some of which are sponsored weekly, monthly and annually and are open to all citizens. A recent example of a city-partnership event is the Blues Festival, co-sponsored with the Brazos Valley African American Heritage and Cultural Society (BVAAHCS). The following statement from a city council member illustrates the city's new attitude: "The Bryan Texas Blues Festival demonstrates the commitment of the City of Bryan to an inclusive tradition of celebrating all aspects of its cultural and musical heritage."

The city's support of Mrs. Mel Pruitt and Willie Pruitt, founders of the Brazos Valley African American Museum that opened in 2006, also demonstrates how Bryan has changed in recent years. The museum has played an important role in helping to bridge the racial gap in Bryan by honoring and recognizing all citizens and their contributions. Willie and Mel served in both the segregated and integrated Bryan Public Schools for a combined total of over seventy-one years. He was a teacher and assistant principal, and she was a teacher, girls' basketball coach and counselor.

The city also has a unique relationship with its neighboring city, College Station, through the Bryan–College Station Convention and Visitors Bureau, the Bryan–College Station Chamber of Commerce Transportation Committee, the Bryan–College Station Metropolitan Planning Organization Board and the Bryan–College Station Metropolitan Planning Organization Technical Advisory Committee. Over the years, the city lines between Bryan and College Station have become almost invisible. As a result, both cities are able to extend to its citizens a wide range of integrated celebrations and events, such as the Juneteenth Legacy, that enhance the cities' diversity in people and resources. Texas Reds' Steak and Grape Festival, one of Bryan's premier festivals, has become international in its reach, attracting several foreign countries since its inception. The Bush Presidential Library Museum in College Station attracts thousands of visitors every year.

AFTERWORD

Having spent the last three or more years thinking, reviewing documents, interviewing, writing and rewriting, I am left to reflect on several issues. While I have no new information or comments to make beyond those made in the text, I would like to recap and add certain points.

First, let's look at what this project was intended to do. This book is about segregated public education and African American life in Bryan, Texas, from the years 1885 to 1971 and includes events as recent as 2012. This book also covers a number of other topics, from local government and elected black officials to black businesses. While all the topics are important, I focused more heavily on education and schools, for they were the fulcrum for all other segregated experiences. Segregation made every facet of life unequal until its removal in 1971.

I tried to point out how segregation created a social climate that pervaded African American life at many different levels. I tried to document and show how inadequate school funding, administration, teacher salary, training and curriculum shaped African American education. But teachers tried to shelter students from the worst damage of segregation and prepare them to be successful—to move forward from behind. They embraced education and encouraged students to see it as the means to freedom. Of all the other topics, education for African Americans was perhaps the most important. It dominated the thoughts of teachers and parents and helped to knock down barriers in the way of success. I believe it can be said without contradiction that education was *sine qua non* in the African American community.

Education offered promise and a chance to fulfill dreams in the absence of material prosperity.

Another objective of this project was to prepare a document that serves as a reminder of the commonly shared education and school experiences from the time period covered in this book. I wanted to highlight the roles that the Bryan Public School for Colored, E.A. Kemp Junior-Senior High, Washington Elementary, George Washington Carver Elementary, E.A. Kemp Senior High and R.C. Neal Junior High played in the lives of hundreds of African American boys and girls. I wanted to show, in spite of the resistant behavior and indifference demonstrated by too many of the majority of citizens, how some boys and girls succeeded. That is not to say that the majority of citizens were indifferent. For example, Mr. and Mrs. D.D. Matthews and Mr. and Mrs. Frank Pierce were decent, and they demonstrated generosity in every way. In writing this book, I learned that certain members of the Fererri, Varisco and Waldrop families, as well as unidentified others, were generous and also helpful to African Americans in Bryan. I learned from some of the individuals interviewed that there were numerous majority families who helped in significant and countless ways.

I tried to show how small African American business owners, as entrepreneurs, helped to create economic independence from local employers and sustain their families. I also tried to show how the small business owners helped to create, directly or indirectly, an attitude of independence by providing jobs to individuals in the community. But there is little doubt that obtaining an education helped African Americans think independently and see themselves as positive and worthy citizens. The section on E.A. Kemp Alumni Academic and Professional Achievements shows that African American students were successful, despite the barriers that segregation imposed upon them.

I tried to show how limited job opportunities created housing needs that resulted in substandard living conditions. Substandard housing ultimately led to the construction of government projects on both sides of the city. I tried to show how others, namely elected officials, made contributions to the community. I tried to point out some of the ironies, contradictions and paradoxes prevalent in the lives of African Americans as a result of segregation in Bryan, Texas. I tried to honor and recognize teachers and parents who, with so little, helped greatly to bring us thus far along the way.

Finally, I set out to write about African American Bryan life during segregation and Bryan's transition using facts, recollections and reflections that encapsulated the hardships of African Americans. Whatever level of success was achieved or whether I succeeded at all must be determined by you, the reader.

BIBLIOGRAPHY

Anderson, F.G., and Wakefield, E.A., eds. *The History of Medicine in Brazos County.* Bryan, TX: self-published, 2001.

Banks, Olivia. "A Remembrance." In *The Sesquicentennial Edition Brazos County History: Rich Past Bright Future*, edited by G.F. Brundige. Bryan, TX: Family Foundation, 2006.

Battle, T.C., and D.M. Wallace, eds. *Legacy: Treasures of Black History.* Washington, D.C.: National Geographic, 2006.

Bethune Woman's Club. *E.A. Kemp High 1885–1985.* Bryan, TX, 1985.

Blair, John. "Volunteer State Guard." *Brazos Guard* (Summer 2005).

Borden, Robert. *Historic Brazos County: An Illustrated History.* San Antonio, TX: Historical Publishing Network, 2005.

Boykin, R.D. *Brazos Valley Italians: A Series of Interviews.* College Station, TX: C&R Publications, 1996.

Brazos County Historical Commission: Black Education in Bryan 1975. Acessed July 28, 1975. www.brazoscountyhistory.org.

Brazos County Historical Time Line from 1800–2000. Accessed July 29, 2012. www.brazosgenealogy.org.

Brundige, G.F., ed. *The Texas Sesquicentennial Edition Brazos County History: Rich Past-Bright Future.* Bryan, TX: Family Foundation, 1986.

Bryan–College Station Eagle, February 8, 1986.

———. "Harris McGee." June 11, 2011. theeagle.com.

———. "Lincoln High Colored School." May 12, 2009. theeagle.com.

Bryan Daily Eagle. "Many White Citizens." March 19, 1939. In *Historic Brazos County: An Illustrated History*, by Robert Borden. San Antonio, TX: Historical Publishing Network, 2005.

———. "Negro Population." March 10, 1939. In *Historic Brazos County: An Illustrated History*, by Robert Borden. San Antonio, TX: Historical Publishing Network, 2005.

———. October 23, 1913. In *Historic Brazos County: An Illustrated History*, by Robert Borden. San Antonio, TX: Historical Publishing Network, 2005.

———. "Old Presbyterian." January 18, 1906. In *Historic Brazos County: An Illustrated History*, by Robert Borden. San Antonio, TX: Historical Publishing Network, 2005.

Bryan Independent School District. Alumni Directory. New York: Bernard C. Harris Publishing Company, 2002.

"Bryan, Texas 1960 Population." Wikipedia. Last modified July 19, 2012. en.wikipedia.org.

Bryan, Texas 2000 Census Information. Last modified July 28, 2012. www.localcencus.com.

Buford, Michael D. *Up from Cotton.* N.p.: n.d.

The City of Bryan, Texas. History of Bryan, Texas. Last modified August 1, 2012. www.bryantx.gov.

City of Bryan, Texas. Ordinance Number 82, Amendment 1. 972.

City of Bryan Website. Directory of Appointed and Elected Officials. July 29, 2012. www.bryantx.gov.

Dorsey, Mary. *Those Were the Days: Bryan, Brazos County, Texas 1821–1921.* Brazos County, TX: 1976.

Farris, Sandra. Bryan High School History. Last modified November 16, 2010. fc.bryanisd.org.

———. History of Bryan ISD. Bryan, TX: Bryan Independent School District. www.bryanisd.org.

Felder, Cain Hope, ed. *Stony the Road We Trod: African Biblical Interpretation.* Minneapolis: Fortress Press, 1991.

Felleman, Hazel. *The Best Loved Poems of the American People.* New York: Doubleday, 1936. Reprint, 1979.

Foster, Betty Clements. *Bryan Legends and Legacies.* Bryan, TX: City of Bryan, 1996.

Foster, Michele. *Black Teachers On Teaching.* New York: New Press, 1997.

From Then Until Now. E.A. Kemp High School Classes of the '50s Reunion Telephone Directory. Bryan, TX: E.A. Kemp High School, 1990.

Gates, Henry Louis, Jr. *Colored People: A Memoir*. New York: Vintage Books, 1994.

Handbook of Texas Online. Last modified date July 30, 2012. www.tshaonline.org/handbook/index.html.

Harley, S. Middleton, and C.M. Stokes. *The African Experience: A History.* Englecliffs, NJ: Globe Book Company, 1992.

Hayre, Ruth Wright. *Tell Them We Are Still Rising: A Memoir of Faith in Education*. New York: Wiley and Sons, 1997.

A History of Bryan Parks and Recreation, 1868–2004. www.bryantx.org.

Holt, John. *Freedom and Beyond*. New York: Dell Publishing Company, 1972.

Hooks, Bell. *Bone Black: Memories of Girlhood*. New York: Henry Holt, 1996.

Hughes, Langston. "In Derrick Bell." *Faces at the Bottom of the Well.* New York: Basic Books, 1994.

———. *Poetry for Young People*. Edited by David Roesse and Arnold Rampersad. New York: Sterling Publishing, 2006.

In Fulfillment of a Dream: African Americans at Texas A and M University. College Station: Texas A&M University, Spring 2001.

Jackson, A.W. *A Sure Foundation: A Sketch of Negro Life in Texas*. 1st ed. Houston, TX: n.d.

The John M. Moore High School Out-Look 1, no. 1 (May 1946).

King, Martin L., Jr. In *Salvation: Black People and Love*, by Bell Hooks. New York: HarperCollins Publishers, 2001.

Kirszer, Laurie G., and Stephen R. Mandell. *Literature*. 3rd ed. New York: Harcourt Brace College Publishers, 1997.

Lowell, James Russell. In *I Have a Dream: Writings and Speeches That Changed the World*, by J.M. Washington. Glenview, IL: Scott Foresman, 1992.

Marshall, Elmer Grady. "The History of Brazos County, Texas." Master's thesis, University of Texas, August 1937.

McGee-Harris, Patsy Ruth. *John M. Moore High School History*. N.p.: n.d.

McKay, P. "Black History." *The Texas Sesquicentennial Edition Brazos County History: Rich Past—Bright Future*. Edited by G.F. Brundige. Bryan, TX: Family Foundation, 1986.

The Men and Women in WW-II from Brazos County and Aggie Veterans. N.p.: n.d.

Nance, Joseph M. *The Early History of Bryan and Surrounding Area*. Bryan, TX: 1962.

Nash, Sunny. *Big Mama Didn't Shop at Woolworth's*. College Station: Texas A&M University Press, 1966.

Ogletree, Charles J. *All Deliberate Speed: Reflections on First Half Century of* Brown v. Board of Education. New York: W.W. Norton and Company, 2004.

Page, Bill. "African Americans in Brazos County, 1840–1865." Last modified May 20, 2012. www.brazosgeneaology.org.

Palmer, Parker J. *The Courage to Teach: Exploring the Inner Landscape of Teachers' Life*. San Francisco, CA: Jossey-Bass Publishers, 1998.

Person, Oswell, and William Kritsonis. *A Brief Analysis of the Historical Development of Higher Education for African Americans*. Houston, TX: National Forum Press, 2006.

Randall, J.G., and David Donald. *The Civil War and Reconstruction*. 2nd ed. Boston: D.C. Heath, 1961.

Renick, James. Inauguration as Chancellor of North Carolina Agricultural and Technical State University.

Sadberry, Oliver W. *Black Education in Brazos County*. N.p.: n.d.

Sowell, Thomas. *Race and Culture: A World View*. New York: HarperCollins Publisher, 1994.

St. Joseph's History Bryan Hospital. Last modified July 29, 2012. www.st.joseph.org.

Swisher, Carl Brent. *American Constitutional Development*. 2nd ed. Cambridge, MA: Riverside Press, 1954.

Texas Constitution 1866, Article 8. tarletonlaw.utexas.edu.

U.S. Bureau of the Census. 2005 Bryan, Texas. Washington, D.C.: Bureau of the Census. www.census.gov.

Watkins, William H. *The White Architects of Black Education: Ideology and Power in America, 1865–1954*. New York: Teachers College Press, Columbia University, 2001.

Wesley, Charles H. *Neglected History: Essays in Negro-American History by a College President*. Washington, D.C.: Association for the Study of Negro Life and History, 1969.

Wilcox, Lois Ayne. "The Early History of Bryan, Texas." Master's thesis, University of Texas, 1952.

Williams, T.H, R.N. Current and A. Freidel. *A History of the United States to 1877*. New York: Alfred A. Knopf, 1996.

INDEX

L

M

N

O

P

R

S

T

U

V

W

Y

ABOUT THE AUTHOR

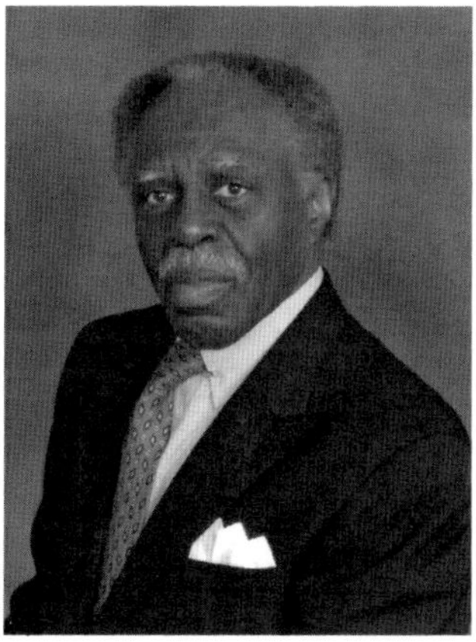

Oswell Person received his early education at Washington Elementary School and at E.A. Kemp Junior-Senior High School in Bryan, Texas. He earned a BS from D.C. Teachers College, an MLS from the University of Maryland and a PhD from Michigan State University. He was also the first African American to serve as campus president of Tarrant County Junior College in Fort Worth, Texas. Person served as president of Oakland Community College–Highland Lakes in Waterford, Michigan, and was interim president of Paul Quinn College in Dallas, Texas. His long list of academic positions includes vice-president of the Office of Academic Affairs at Jarvis Christian College in Hawkins, Texas; dean of the Center of Common Studies and director of Learning Resources in Santa Clara, California; dean of Telecommunication and the Arts; dean of Student Personnel Services at Lansing Community College in Lansing, Michigan; and associate professor of education at Prairie View A&M University in Prairie View, Texas. He is also the author of *Moving Forward from Behind* and coauthor of *A Brief Analysis of the Historical Development of Higher Education for African Americans*.

He is married to the former Constance Y. Harpole of Los Angeles, California, who earned both her BA and MA degrees from Howard University, an MA from Santa Clara University and an EdD from the University of San Francisco. They have two adult sons: Erick Christopher, who resides in Washington, D.C., and Stephen, who resides in Fort Worth, Texas.